SMART SOCIAL AND MONEY SKILLS FOR TEENS

2 IN 1 EASY GUIDE TO IMPROVE COMMUNICATION, MANAGE SOCIAL ANXIETY, BOOST FINANCIAL LITERACY FOR A MORE CONFIDENT AND INDEPENDENT TEEN

SYDNEY PARKER

SOCIAL SKILLS FOR TEENS MADE EASY: STEP-BY-STEP GUIDE TO IMPROVE COMMUNICATION, MAKE FRIENDS, MANAGE SOCIAL ANXIETY, AND BUILD CONFIDENCE IN 30 DAYS, EVEN IF YOU ARE SELF-CONSCIOUS

INTRODUCTION

Have you ever felt like you're on the outside looking in? Maybe you've been at a party, clutching a solo cup and wishing you knew just what to say, or perhaps you've sat through a group project feeling like you're the only one who just can't jump into the conversation. If any of this sounds familiar, you're not alone.

Once, during my own high school years, I found myself sweating bullets at a school dance, unable to muster the courage to talk to anyone. It wasn't until a kind soul, seeing my distress, reached out with a simple "Hey, it's louder here than a concert, right?" that I realized all it took was a moment, a phrase, to break the ice. That night wasn't just about survival; it was a stepping stone in my journey toward mastering the world of social interaction.

Indeed, I've been right where you are. My own journey through the maze of communication has given me a wealth of understanding to share. This book represents the best of what I've learned, driven by my desire to guide you through the complex social landscape. I've played every part—the quiet one on the sidelines, the one leading the conversation, and everything in between, from battling nerves to embracing confidence. I'm here to share the insights I've gathered with you.

"Social Skills for Teens Made Easy: Step-by-Step Guide to Improve Communication, Make Friends, Manage Social Anxiety, and Build Confidence in 30 Days, Even if You Are Self-Conscious" is designed with you in mind. Over the next 30 days, you will embark on a transformative journey. Each day, you'll be met with a reflective journal prompt, engaging activities, or a fun and tailored quiz to help you grow. We'll cover everything from the basics of making small talk to the finer points of digital etiquette.

This book isn't just a guide; it's a conversation—a conversation that understands the laughs and struggles of being a teenager. Whether you're dealing with a racing heart at the thought of speaking up in class or just looking for ways to expand your circle of friends, this book has something for you. I've included stories from well-known personalities who, just like you, faced their own social challenges and came out stronger on the other side.

As we dive into the various sections, each themed to tackle different aspects of social skills—from understanding your emotions to stepping up as a leader—you'll find this book is your ally. It's written to guide you through the sometimes overwhelming landscape of social interactions, providing clear, actionable steps and celebrating every little victory along the way.

So, whether you consider yourself shy or just socially curious, I invite you to turn the page and take the first step. Let's unlock your potential together, one day at a time. Ready to start? Why not turn that social anxiety into social prowess and transform those awkward moments into stories you'll one day share as triumphs? Welcome to a journey of becoming the best version of yourself.

SECTION 1: BUILDING A FOUNDATION OF SELF-CONFIDENCE

"I've had my doubts. I've had a lot of moments when I didn't feel confident enough to take a role, and I didn't know if I could do it."

EMMA WATSON

Have you been in a situation where it felt like you're the only one who didn't get the memo? Like, maybe everyone else attended a secret workshop titled "How to Be Smooth and Effortlessly Cool 101"? You're not alone in feeling this way, and guess what? The secret to breaking through this invisible barrier isn't found in having a fire haircut or knowing the right people. It starts inside your head, with what you tell yourself daily.

The not-so-secret sauce to growing your social prowess is self-confidence; a big chunk of that comes from your conversations with yourself. Yes, I'm talking about the voice in your head that either pumps you up or drags you down. In this section, we're going to turn down the volume on that inner critic and tune into a channel that's more like your own personal hype station. Ready to flip the switch? Let's crank up the confidence with some positive self-talk vibes.

~

DAY 1 THE POWER OF POSITIVE SELF-TALK: REWIRING THOUGHTS

First, let's shine a light on that sneaky culprit known as negative self-talk. It's like a background app on your phone that slowly drains your battery; you might not even notice it's there, but it's sapping your power all the same. Phrases like "I can't do this" or "I'm not good enough" are classic hits on the negative self-talk chart-toppers. But where do these thoughts come from? Often, they're the echoes of past criticisms or failures, and our brain keeps replaying them, trying to protect us from future flops.

Now, how do you switch tracks from these downer tunes to something more upbeat? Here are some DJ tricks for your brain: affirmation exercises and thought substitution. Affirmations are like your personal cheerleading squad chanting positive statements about your abilities and worth. Start with something simple like, "I am capable of more than I realize," and say it with conviction, preferably in front of a mirror. Thought substitution means catching those negative thoughts in the act and swapping them out with a positive or realistic one. Think of it as switching from a sad playlist to a hype playlist.

Let's put this into practice. Suppose someone criticizes your project in class. Instead of spiraling into "I'm terrible at this," pause and flip the script. Remind yourself, "I can learn from this feedback," or "Everyone has off days." By regularly practicing these swaps, you'll find that positive thoughts start to come more naturally, like getting better at a video game the more you play.

Consistently choosing positive thoughts can transform more than just your momentary mood. Research shows that a positive outlook can lead to better stress management, enhanced problem-solving, and improved relationships—all essential for successful social interactions. Think of it as upgrading your mental software to run more efficiently in social settings, making you not just a participant in conversations but a confident contributor.

Armed with these tools, you're well on your way to silencing those nagging doubts and amplifying the thoughts that elevate you. Remember, the goal here isn't to never have a negative thought again—that's nearly impossible. Instead, it's about recognizing those thoughts for what they are: just thoughts, not facts. With practice, you'll start to notice a shift not only in how you think but in how you act and interact. Who knows? Maybe at the next school dance, you'll offer a shy peer a comforting word, turning their evening around just like someone did for mine. Keep tuning into your new mental playlist, and let the good vibes roll!

Journal Entry Prompt:

How did it feel to identify and challenge your negative thoughts today? Reflect on a specific moment when a negative thought arose. What did you tell yourself to counter it? Did you notice any immediate changes in your emotions or physical sensations? How did this shift impact the rest of your day, interactions, or decisions? Consider whether you found it easier or harder to stay positive as the day progressed.

_____

_____

_____

_____

_____

DAY 2 UNDERSTANDING YOUR SELF-WORTH: BEYOND THE MIRROR

Let's talk about mirrors—not just the ones you use to check your hair or practice those TikTok dance moves. I mean the metaphorical mirrors that reflect how we see ourselves. Often, what we see doesn't just come from us. It's a collage of opinions, expectations, and the glossy, filtered snapshots of people's lives we scroll through daily. But here's the kicker: understanding your self-worth is like realizing that you're the artist, not just the canvas. You get to decide which influences to brush onto your self-image and which ones don't make the cut.

First up, let's do a little inventory of your awesomeness. Yes, you've got strengths and achievements worth celebrating, even if they might not all be trophy-and-ribbon material. Maybe you're the friend everyone knows will keep their secrets, or perhaps you have a knack for making people laugh when they need it most. These qualities are gold. So, grab a pen and paper, or open a new note on your phone, and start listing things you're good at and moments you've felt proud of yourself. Big or small, write them all. This isn't just feel-good fluff; it's about recognizing the unique mix of traits and successes that make you, well, you.

Now, let's tackle those sneaky negative perceptions. We've all got them, and they often stem from comparing ourselves to others—thanks, social media. Say you see someone acing a test or getting tons of likes on a post, and suddenly you feel like you're not measuring up. Here's a technique to try: reframe your thinking. Instead of "I'm not as smart as them," how about "Everyone has their strengths, and I'm working on mine"? Or swap "I'll never be that popular" with "I value genuine connections, and I'm loved by my friends." This isn't about putting on rose-colored glasses; it's about adjusting your focus to give yourself a fair shot.

Choosing role models thoughtfully can also boost your sense of self-worth. Pick out people who reflect the kind of authenticity and values you admire, not just those with the most followers or fame. These might be athletes who've overcome adversity, artists who defy norms, or leaders who stand up for what's right. Think about how their journeys resonate with your own values and aspirations. What qualities do they have that you see in yourself or want to develop? Let their stories remind you that everyone has struggles and that overcoming them is part of what can make you great.

Lastly, let's get real about the filters—not the Instagram kind, but the cultural and social filters that shape how we see ourselves and others. Our world is loud with messages telling us how to look, act, and feel. It's a lot. But here's a thought: what if you could curate these influences as carefully as you curate your social media feed? Start by noticing which messages make you feel good about yourself and which make you doubt your worth. Lean into the books, shows, music, podcasts, and even friend groups that lift you up and reflect the diverse, beautiful reality of the world—not a photoshopped version of perfection.

You're taking control of your self-worth by actively choosing how you see yourself and what influences you let in. It's not always easy, but it's definitely worth it. So next time you catch your reflection—in a mirror, a window, or the eyes of someone who cares about you—remember that you're seeing a work in progress, a masterpiece that's all your own. Keep painting, refining, and stepping back to admire how far you've come.

Quiz: Understanding Your Self-Worth

1. What are metaphorical mirrors?
   a. Physical mirrors used to check your fabulous hair
   b. Opinions and expectations that reflect how we see ourselves
   c. Social media selfies
2. Why is it important to recognize your personal strengths?
   a. To compare them with others, like a competition
   b. To celebrate and build a positive self-image like a boss
   c. To win shiny trophies and ribbons

3. What should you do when you notice negative self-talk?
   a. Ignore it like background noise
   b. Accept it as accurate because why not
   c. Challenge it and replace it with a positive thought, like a mental ninja
4. Which of the following is an example of a positive affirmation?
   a. "I'm not as cool as others"
   b. "Everyone has their strengths, and I'm working on mine"
   c. "I'll never be that popular, so why try?"
5. How can choosing role models thoughtfully impact your self-worth?
   a. It can make you feel like a potato
   b. It can inspire you to develop qualities you admire and become a superhero
   c. It has no impact on self-worth because who cares
6. What should you do about cultural and social messages that make you doubt your worth?
   a. Ignore all messages and become a hermit
   b. Curate influences that make you feel good about yourself, like a personal DJ
   c. Accept all messages as gospel truth
7. True or False: Understanding your self-worth means never having negative thoughts again.
   a. True, you'll be like a positivity robot
   b. False, because even superheroes have off days

Answer Key:

1. b) Opinions and expectations that reflect how we see ourselves

2. b) To celebrate and build a positive self-image like a boss

3. c) Challenge it and replace it with a positive thought, like a mental ninja

4. b) "Everyone has their strengths, and I'm working on mine"

5. b) It can inspire you to develop qualities you admire and become a superhero

6. b) Curate influences that make you feel good about yourself, like a personal DJ

7. b) False, because even superheroes have off days

DAY 3 SETTING ACHIEVABLE GOALS: SMALL STEPS TO BIG CHANGES

Imagine playing a video game where the final boss seems light years away, and you're just armed with a beginner's toolkit. It seems daunting, right? Well, setting life goals can sometimes feel just as intimidating, especially when the endgame is something as big as "Become the most charismatic person at school" or "Ace all my courses this semester." But fear not! Just like in video games, there's a strategy to leveling up in real life, too. It's called setting SMART goals. SMART stands for Specific, Measurable, Achievable, Relevant, and Time-bound. Each goal you set should be a clear and achievable mini-mission within a specific time frame.

Let's break it down with a common teen scenario: improving your grades in math. A SMART goal would be, "I will improve my math grade from a B to an A by the end of the semester by practicing math problems for at least 30 minutes each day." See how specific and time-bound that is? It's not just "get better at math"—which is as vague as saying "be more awesome." It's precise, giving you a clear target to hit and a way to measure your progress.

Now, let's talk about breaking down larger goals. Say you want to become more socially active. That's a marathon, not a sprint, and it's about adding layers of interactions, not diving into the deep end without a life jacket. Start small. Your first goal might be, "I will start a conversation with one new person each week for a month." Each conversation is a step towards that larger goal. Think of each small goal as a checkpoint in your favorite game. You're not just running aimlessly; you're passing these checkpoints and gaining the confidence to move on to the next level.

Consistency and patience are your best friends in this game. It's like building muscle. If you've ever tried to lift weights, you know you don't just start by bench pressing 200 pounds. You start small, stay consistent, and gradually build up your strength. The same goes for any skill, including social skills. There might be days when it feels like you are making no progress at all or like you're the awkward turtle at the party. That's okay. Every expert was once a beginner. Keep at it, keep setting small, achievable goals, and you'll find that you're building not just skills but confidence.

And here's the fun part: celebrating milestones. Let's say you've managed to talk to a new person each week for a month. That's a milestone! Celebrate it. Consider treating yourself to a movie night out or a small party with close friends. These celebrations act like save points in your journey, moments to reflect on how far you've come and recharge your batteries for the next leg of the adventure. They remind you that progress is still progress, no matter how small. And when you look back, all those small steps will add up to a giant leap towards your bigger goals.

As you set out to conquer your personal quests, remember that the path to achieving big changes is through setting small, manageable, SMART goals. Keep your objectives clear and your actions consistent, and don't forget to celebrate your victories. Each small step is a piece of the puzzle in completing the grand picture of your aspirations. And before you know it, you'll look back amazed at the distance you've covered, one SMART goal at a time.

Activity: Setting Achievable Goals. Create a SMART Goal

Identify a Goal: Think of something you want to achieve socially, like making new friends or joining a club.

Make it SMART:
- Specific: Define your goal clearly.
- Measurable: Decide how you'll track progress.
- Achievable: Ensure it's realistic.
- Relevant: Make sure it matters to you.
- Time-bound: Set a deadline.

Example Goal: "I will start a conversation with one new person each week for the next month to build my social skills and confidence, beginning with classmates and gradually moving to new acquaintances."

Write down your SMART goal and review it regularly!

DAY 4 CONSTRUCTIVE SELF-CRITIQUE: GROWING FROM FEEDBACK

Let's face it: getting feedback can sometimes feel like swallowing a spoonful of cough syrup. It might not always taste great, but it's supposed to help you get better, right? The trick is in knowing how to tell the difference between feedback that's like that beneficial, although bitter, syrup, and the kind that's just plain bitter. Understanding this can transform potentially discouraging experiences into powerful growth moments.

Constructive criticism is like a personal trainer for your skills—it's meant to challenge and strengthen you, not tear you down. It focuses on specific actions or behaviors rather than attacking you as a person. For example, if a teacher comments, "Your essay had some interesting points, but the arguments could be clearer with more supporting evidence," that's constructive. It's clear, specific, and aimed at helping you improve. On the flip side, destructive criticism often feels like a low blow. It's vague and personal, something like, "Your essay was terrible." There's nothing to learn from here; it's just disparaging.

When you receive constructive criticism, think of it as a cheat code to level up. The first step in taking feedback gracefully is to listen—really listen—without rushing to defend yourself. It's about keeping your cool and staying open to the possibility that there's room for improvement. Let's say your soccer coach suggests you need to work on your passing skills. Instead of getting defensive, a simple "Thanks, I'll practice that" can go a long way. Later, when you're on your own, you can process what was said. Reflect on the feedback objectively: What's the core message? How can it help me improve? This reflection turns input into a tool rather than a weapon.

Self-evaluation is like doing a reality check on yourself. It's about stepping back and looking at your performance with a clear, unbiased eye. Start by asking yourself some reflective questions: What went well in that presentation? What didn't go as planned? Why? Be honest with yourself, but also be kind. The goal here isn't to beat yourself up but to figure out your strengths and where you could use a little boost. It's also about recognizing that growth is a continuous process. Every step forward, no matter how small, is progress.

Another great technique is to set up your own 'feedback sessions' with yourself. After completing a task or reaching a milestone, take a moment to jot down what you learned, what you could have done differently, and how you can apply this knowledge in the future. This habit not only cements what you've learned but also prepares you to handle external feedback better because you've already assessed yourself.

Now, for the fun part—turning feedback into action. This is where the magic happens. Start by breaking down the feedback into actionable steps. If your debate coach says you need to work on your rebuttals, plan specific ways to improve, like watching skilled debaters in action or practicing with a teammate. Create a mini-action plan: What will you do? When will you do it? How often? By breaking it down into smaller, manageable tasks, the feedback becomes less daunting and more doable.

Remember, the goal of feedback is improvement, not perfection. It's about getting better, step by step. Each piece of advice is a stepping stone to becoming more skilled, knowledgeable, and, yes, more confident in your abilities. So, next time you receive feedback, embrace it like a secret tip-off in your favorite game. It might just be the clue that leads you to your next big win.

As you continue to navigate through your teen years, remember that feedback is not something to dread but something to welcome with open arms. It's the magic ingredient in the recipe for personal growth and success. Embrace each piece of advice, each constructive critique, as a golden opportunity to refine your skills and develop into the person you aspire to be. Keep pushing forward, keep refining, and most importantly, keep growing. Your future self will thank you for it.

Activity: Constructive Self-Critique

Learn to distinguish constructive criticism from destructive criticism and use feedback for personal growth. Use the space provided below.

Identify feedback: Think of a recent piece of feedback you received. Write it down.

Analyze the Feedback: Determine if the feedback was constructive or destructive.

Constructive feedback example: "Your presentation was good, but you could improve by speaking more slowly."

Destructive feedback example: "Your presentation was terrible."

Reflect and Plan: Reflect on the constructive feedback. Ask yourself, "What can I learn from this?"

Create a mini-action plan to improve based on the feedback. For example, "I will practice speaking slowly in front of a mirror for 10 minutes each day."

By distinguishing and reflecting on feedback, you can turn it into a powerful tool for personal growth.

_____

_____

_____

_____

_____

CELEBRATING SMALL VICTORIES: KEEPING A VICTORY JOURNAL

Imagine every small win celebrated like a championship victory—crowd roaring, confetti flying. That's the essence of a victory journal. It's your personal space to acknowledge and celebrate daily achievements, making you the MVP of your own life. A victory journal is simply a record of your successes, big or small, from mastering a challenging subject to forming a new friendship. It serves as a tangible reminder of your capabilities, acting as your personal cheerleader and boosting your confidence whenever doubts arise.

Guidelines for Effective Journaling

Effective journaling captures your experiences and feelings in any form that resonates with you—be it bullet points, sketches, or stickers. Focus on the details. For instance, rather than merely noting, "Talked to a new classmate," delve into how you felt before, during, and after the conversation. Did you experience a surge of joy? Documenting these nuances helps you appreciate your achievements when revisiting your entries. Consistency matters. Although daily entries aren't mandatory, establishing a routine like a weekly check-in can maintain your momentum. Think of this as your opportunity to celebrate the week's accomplishments and reflect on your growth.

Celebrating Small Victories

Everything that makes you proud qualifies as a victory. Whether it's participating in class, initiating a conversation, or maintaining positivity through tough times, each achievement is a step forward in your personal development journey and deserves recognition. Even subtle wins, like avoiding negative interactions or adhering to your study plan, are significant markers of your resilience and growth.

The Power of Reflection

A victory journal is more than a record; it's a reflective tool that highlights your evolving confidence and skills. Regular reviews can reveal progress and patterns, such as increased ease in social situations or the formation of new friendships. This process not only celebrates your journey but also aids in setting future goals. Recognizing past successes can boost your confidence to take on new challenges, from joining clubs to leading projects. Incorporating victory journaling into your routine underscores your continuous achievements and development. It transforms your journey into a celebration of progress, encouraging you to acknowledge and build upon your successes.

Activity:

Secure a notebook or journal for your entries. If cost is a concern, opt for a free digital app or repurpose any available notebook. This will be your space for reflection and goal setting.

From the smallest seed, a resilient tree begins its journey, rooting itself firmly in the earth. Like self-confidence, it starts small but holds the promise of growth and strength, nourished by the belief in one's potential.

SECTION 2: OVERCOMING SOCIAL ANXIETY

"I think my nerves come from a place of feeling like I want to give it my all. But as I've gotten older, I've realized that everyone feels that way, and you just have to push through it."

EMMA STONE

W alking into a room and suddenly feeling like your brain has turned into that annoying buggering icon on a slow internet day? Your heart's racing, your palms are sweaty, and you're pretty sure if someone spoke to you, you'd accidentally spit out your last Google search instead of a greeting. Welcome to the wild world of social anxiety. It's like your brain's natural fight or flight response is a superhero that thinks every social interaction is a villain. But don't worry, even superheroes have their off days, and this section is all about turning your social anxiety from a supernuisance into your superpower.

∼

UNDERSTANDING SOCIAL ANXIETY: THE WHAT AND WHY

According to Merriam-Webster, social anxiety is "a form of anxiety that occurs in social situations where one fears being judged or scrutinized by others." This feeling of nervousness or fear can make everyday interactions feel overwhelming for many teens. It's like feeling butterflies in your stomach, but a lot more intense. But remember, it's something many people experience, and there are ways to manage it and feel more confident.

Social anxiety often stems from embarrassing or stressful past experiences. It's amplified by pressures from social media and the high academic expectations placed on teens today. These factors can make social situations feel overwhelming.

This condition can follow you beyond school, affecting your willingness to engage in social activities and impacting your academic performance and relationships. It's like being a spectator in your own life, present but not fully participating.

Contrary to some beliefs, social anxiety is common among teens and possible to overcome. It doesn't mean changing who you are; instead, it means learning to feel more comfortable in your own skin. Knowing what social anxiety is, its triggers, and how it affects you is the first step toward regaining control. It's about learning to navigate through your anxiety, not waiting for it to disappear. Let's prepare to lower the volume of your anxiety and amplify your life instead.

Harness the overlooked superpower of your breath to counteract social anxiety. Diaphragmatic or belly breathing is a simple yet effective method to induce calmness, shifting from panic to peace by activating your body's relaxation response.

Quick Guide to Belly Breathing

Find a Quiet Space: Sit or lie down in a comfortable position.

Position Your Hands: One on your chest, the other on your belly.

Inhale Slowly: Through your nose, allowing your belly to rise more than your chest. Count to four.

Exhale Gradually: Through your mouth for six counts, focusing on the hand on your belly to ensure proper diaphragm engagement.

Tools: Visual aids and apps can enhance your practice.

Utilize belly breathing before social situations or whenever anxiety creeps in. It's a subtle, powerful technique to armor yourself against stress. It's beneficial both as an immediate calm-provider and a long-term resilience builder.

Incorporating this practice daily can remarkably reduce anxiety, boost concentration, improve sleep quality, and elevate your overall well-being. It equips you with the confidence to navigate social interactions, helping to transform anxiety into manageable serenity.

~

DAY 5 BUILDING A SUPPORT SYSTEM: FINDING YOUR ALLIES

Imagine trying to play a team sport all by yourself. Sounds pretty harsh, right? That's a bit like what dealing with social anxiety can feel like when you're going solo. Having a solid support system is like having the ultimate backup team; it's necessary when tackling the big plays or even just the daily grind. This network isn't just about having people to hang out with—it's about building a team that can pass you the ball when you're blocked, cheer you on when you make that game-winning shot, and help you strategize when you're up against formidable opponents in the form of anxiety.

Now, identifying these allies might feel a bit like scouting for talent. You need people who understand the game you're playing—those who get what it's like to feel anxious in social settings or are empathetic enough to support you even if they don't fully understand the experience. These allies could be friends who notice when you're feeling overwhelmed and can step in with a distraction or a quick escape route. Family members who give you space when you need it but are there to listen when you're ready to talk are invaluable. Even teachers or counselors who recognize your struggle and can provide professional guidance or just a safe space to breathe can be part of this support squad.

So, how do you put this team together? Start by opening up about what you're dealing with. It might be tempting to keep your feelings under wraps, but letting people in is like sending out a signal flare. You'd be surprised how many people are ready and willing to stand by you once they understand what you're facing. Reach out to those you trust and try expressing what kind of support you need, whether it's someone to talk to when you're feeling anxious, someone who can accompany you to social events, or just someone who understands your need for occasional solitude. It's like instructing your teammates on the best plays that can help you win; "Hey, I feel really anxious in large groups. Could we hang out somewhere quieter?" or "I get nervous talking in class. Could you help me practice?"

Building this support system is staying ahead of the game, not just playing catch-up. Why not create a buddy system or a small group among your peers who share similar experiences with anxiety? This can be your go-to group for discussing what's working (or not), sharing strategies, and just having each other's backs. It's about creating a community where everyone speaks the same language of understanding and support, a mutual fan club where everyone is rooting for each other. This isn't just about leaning on others; it's about building mutual support where you are all allies for each other, sharing the load and lifting each other up.

This kind of network doesn't just buffer against the impacts of social anxiety; it actively enhances your overall mental wellness. Each interaction within a supportive group can reinforce the feeling that you are not alone, that others share your experiences or at least understand them, and that support is always at hand. It's about transforming your social anxiety from a solo struggle into a team effort, where every player has a vital role in supporting each other. So, start scouting for your team, reach out for support, build those connections, and strengthen your mutual support systems. With the right people around you, social anxiety can become just another opponent you know how to outplay together.

Journal Prompt: Building Your Support System

Reflect on the people in your life who make you

feel understood and supported. Who are your current allies, and how have they helped you manage social anxiety or difficult situations? Write about one person who has been particularly supportive and describe a specific instance where their support made a difference. Then, think about areas where you might need more support and brainstorm ways to build or strengthen your support system. How can you reach out and communicate your needs to others?

_____

_____

_____

_____

_____

DAY 6 MINDFULNESS IN ACTION: STAYING PRESENT IN SOCIAL SITUATIONS

Do you sometimes find yourself zoning out in the middle of a conversation or worrying about all the ways you could potentially embarrass yourself at the next school event?

That's your brain, the drama queen, taking you on a needless anxiety trip. Here's where mindfulness, your chill cousin, steps in. Mindfulness is all about living in the now, not in the "what ifs" or the reruns of past embarrassments. It's like having a mental remote control that helps you switch off the unnecessary drama and tune into what's happening right in front of you. By focusing on the present, you give less power to your anxiety and more power to yourself in managing how you feel and react in social settings.

Mindfulness isn't just some fancy buzzword; it's a practical tool. For instance, say you're at a party and start feeling overwhelmed by the noise and the number of people. A quick mindfulness exercise could be focusing entirely on a conversation with a person next to you. Listen to their words, notice their expressions, and engage actively. This focused attention helps anchor you in the moment, pushing out anxiety and making the social interaction more manageable and enjoyable. Another simple practice is the "5-4-3-2-1" technique, where you quickly ground yourself by naming five things you can see, four you can touch, three you can hear, two you can smell, and one you can taste. It's like hitting the reset button on your nervous system, pulling your mind away from anxiety triggers and back to reality.

Integrating mindfulness into your daily routine can start small. Maybe begin by spending a few minutes each morning doing nothing but listening to the sounds around you. Or, try mindful walking on your way to school, where you focus entirely on the experience of walking, feeling your feet hit the ground, noticing your breath, and observing what's around you without judgment. Making mindfulness a regular practice can help lower your baseline level of anxiety, making those spike moments of panic less intense. It's like training your mind to be a calm, cool observer of your own life, giving you the power to enjoy each moment more fully.

Let's look at some real-life examples. Consider Jamie, a teen who always felt like an outsider in social situations, worried about saying the wrong thing or not fitting in. By practicing mindfulness, Jamie learned to focus on the flow of interactions rather than over-analyzing every word. This shift allowed for more natural conversations and, surprisingly, more invitations to hang out.

Then there's Morgan, who used mindfulness to manage performance anxiety during school presentations. By focusing on the present moment, Morgan could concentrate on the message rather than the fear of audience judgment, leading to more confident and compelling presentations.

These stories underscore that mindfulness isn't about being perfect or never feeling anxious; it's about managing life's stresses in real time, giving you the tools to stay present and connected, even when anxiety tries to hijack the moment. Whether you're dealing with daily social interactions or specific anxiety-inducing events, mindfulness offers a way to navigate through them with greater ease and confidence. So next time you feel overwhelmed, remember that mindfulness is just a breath away. Practice it, embrace it, and watch how it transforms your experiences, one moment at a time.

Quiz: Answer the following questions to see how well you can wield the power of mindfulness like a social superhero.

1. What is mindfulness?
   a. Reliving your most embarrassing moments on repeat
   b. Staying in the present, like a Zen master

c. Stressing over next week's math test

2. How can mindfulness help you at a party?
   a. By turning you into a social ninja, fully engaged and present
   b. By letting you teleport home
   c. By making you the loudest person in the room

3. Which mindfulness technique is like a superhero's sensory scan?
   a. "5-4-3-2-1" technique
   b. "Counting sheep" (Zzzz...)
   c. "Mindful moonwalking"

4. What's your mission during a mindfulness exercise at a noisy party?
   a. Tune into the noise and start a solo dance party
   b. Worry about saying something silly
   c. Become a conversation superhero by focusing entirely on the person next to you

5. How can you sneak mindfulness into your daily routine?
   a. Walk to school like you're in a zombie apocalypse
   b. Crank up your tunes and block out the world
   c. Play detective: Listen to morning sounds and soak in your surroundings

6. How did Jamie level up social interactions with mindfulness?
   a. Overanalyzed every word like a mad scientist
   b. Focused on the flow of interactions like a social surfer
   c. Avoided social scenes like a ninja in hiding

Answer Key:

1. b) Staying in the present, like a Zen master

2. a) By turning you into a social ninja, fully engaged and present
3. a) "5-4-3-2-1" technique
4. c) Become a conversation superhero by focusing entirely on the person next to you
5. c) Play detective: Listen to morning sounds and soak in your surroundings
6. b) Focused on the flow of interactions like a social surfer

～

DAY 7 ROLE-PLAYING SCENARIOS: PRACTICING SOCIAL INTERACTIONS

Imagine you're gearing up for a big game—let's say, the championship of socializing. Just like in sports, you wouldn't jump into the final match without a bit of practice and a game plan, right? That's where role-playing swoops in. It's like your personal social skills gym, where you can flex those interaction muscles in a no-risk environment. Think of it as a rehearsal for real-life social events, where slipping up is part of the process and not a social catastrophe.

Role-playing is a fantastic method to experiment with different social interactions because it lets you navigate various scenarios in a controlled, safe setting. It's a space where mistakes are not only allowed but are expected—it's all part of the learning curve. You can try out different ways to start a conversation, handle a tricky social situation, or even learn how to exit a chat without that awkward "umm, I gotta go water my cat" excuse. The beauty of role-playing is that it builds your confidence. The more you practice, the less scary real-life interactions become. You start to realize that social slip-ups aren't the end of the world—they're just stepping stones to becoming more able to navigate the social sphere.

Let's dive into crafting these scenarios. Start with situations that are common but might stir up a bit of anxiety. Picture walking into a party where you only know the host or tackling a group project where you need to collaborate with classmates you've never spoken to before. How about the classic: making new friends during lunch? By setting the stage for these interactions, you can script out potential dialogues and responses. For instance, what are some ways to break the ice? How might you ask someone about their interests without coming off as too intense? Role-playing allows you to explore these questions in a low-pressure environment, tweaking your approach as you go.

Feedback is a golden nugget in role-playing. It's like having a coach who points out what moves are scoring points and where you might need to tweak your strategy. This feedback should be constructive and focused on specific behaviors, not just a pat on the back or a vague "that was weird." For example, if your voice tends to get really high when you're nervous, your role-play partner can point that out, and you can work on keeping your tone more relaxed. Or maybe you tend to talk over people when you get excited. Feedback will help you recognize these habits so you can consciously keep them in check.

Starting with more straightforward interactions is the key. You wouldn't lift the heaviest weights on your first day at the gym, and the same goes for social role-playing. Begin with scenarios that feel slightly uncomfortable but doable. As your confidence muscles grow stronger, you can gradually increase the complexity of the interactions. Maybe start with asking a classmate about a homework assignment and work your way up to debating a topic in front of the class. Each step up takes you further out of your comfort zone and deeper into becoming a social pro.

Through role-playing, you're not just learning about how to handle specific situations; you're also learning about yourself —your strengths, your nervous ticks, and how you react under social pressure. This self-awareness is a critical component of personal growth. It will serve you well beyond high school halls and college campuses. So, step into the role-play arena, try on different social hats, and discover the best ways to express yourself. Each scenario is a scene in the great play of your social life, and you're the star—it's time to act like it!

Activity: Role-Playing Scenarios - Tackling a Group Project

Objective: Use role-playing to practice collaborating with classmates you've never spoken to before.

Gather a Partner: Find a friend or family member to role-play with you.
Set the Scene: Imagine you're in a classroom, and you've been assigned to a group project with classmates you don't know well.
Role-Play Scenario 1: Introducing Yourself
- You: "Hi everyone, I'm [Your Name]. I'm excited to work on this project with you all. What do you think about starting with brainstorming ideas?"
Role-Play Scenario 2: Discussing Roles
- You: "I have some ideas for the project outline.

Does anyone have a preference for specific tasks? I can handle the research part if that works for everyone."

Give feedback: After each scenario, your partner gives constructive feedback on your introduction and collaboration approach. Focus on specifics like tone of voice, clarity, and engagement.

Reflect: Write down one thing you learned and one thing you want to work on.

Example: "I felt more confident introducing myself. Next time, I'll try to ask more open-ended questions to involve everyone."

As we wrap up this section on overcoming social anxiety, remember that the strategies discussed here are tools in your toolkit. From understanding what social anxiety really is, building a supportive network, and mastering calming techniques like deep breathing and mindfulness to practicing through role-playing—each strategy offers a unique way to manage and eventually minimize the impact of anxiety in your social life.

Armed with these tools, you're better equipped to face the social challenges ahead with confidence and poise. As we transition into the next section, we'll explore how to further enhance these skills, ensuring that you're not just surviving social interactions but genuinely thriving in them.

As the tree sprouts its first leaves, it begins to stretch towards the sky, breaking through the confines of its shell. Overcoming social anxiety is much like this, a gradual but steady reaching out toward the light of connection and understanding.

SECTION 3: MASTERING COMMUNICATION SKILLS

"Just be yourself, there is no one better."

TAYLOR SWIFT

Picture this: You're at a bustling party, or maybe it's just lunchtime in the cafeteria. You spot someone you've wanted to chat with for ages. They're sipping on their drink or maybe picking at their food, and there's a golden window of opportunity. What do you do? If your plan so far has been to blend into the wallpaper and hope they notice your awesome shirt, let's just put that plan on hold. It's time to level up your convo skills, and this section is like your personal trainer for communication muscles you didn't even know you had.

Starting conversations and keeping them flowing aren't just skills for late-night talk show hosts or politicians; they're essential tools for, well, everyone! Whether you're trying to make new friends, impress your crush, or simply get through a family dinner without awkward silence, you need to master the art of conversation. So, buckle up! We're about to dive into the nuts and bolts of chatting like a champ.

≈

DAY 8 ART OF CONVERSATION: STARTING ENGAGING DIALOGUES

Let's kick things off with how actually to start a conversation. Initiating dialogue can be as nerve-wracking as a squirrel on its first espresso, but it doesn't have to be. The secret? Open-ended questions. These are the kinds of questions that require more than a yes or no answer. They're your golden ticket to a flowing conversation. For instance, instead of asking, "Did you like the movie?" (to which they can reply simply "yes" or "no"), try "What did you think about the movie?" This version invites them to share more, and just like that, you're off to the races.

Using current topics or events as conversation starters is another smooth move. It could be as simple as, "Hey, did you catch the game last night?" or "What did you think of that science presentation today?" It's about finding common ground quickly and hitching your wagon there. Remember, the goal is to get the conversation rolling. You're the spark; what follows could be a delightful dialogue fire!

Now that you've started, let's keep the ball rolling. The objective here is to show genuine interest. People love talking about their interests and experiences, and showing that you care about what they're saying not only keeps the conversation going but also makes it more enjoyable. Follow-up questions are your best friends here. If they mention they play guitar, follow up with, "How did you get started with that?" or "What's your favorite song to play?" Each question opens up a new branch in the conversation tree, and before you know it, you're swinging from topic to topic like a pro.

Sharing related stories or experiences is another way to deepen the conversation. It's like a lively chat over coffee; they share a story, and you respond with one of your own. This back-and-forth keeps the conversation balanced and engaging. Just make sure not to hijack the dialogue; it's about sharing the stage, not performing a solo!

Ah, the dreaded awkward silence. It sometimes sneaks up like a ninja right in the middle of a chat. Don't panic! Use it as a moment to regroup. One way to break the silence is by changing the subject. It's like hitting the refresh button. You could jump to a new topic with something like, "Speaking of movies, have you seen any good ones recently?" Or even use the pause to compliment them: "By the way, I really like your jacket. Where did you get it?" Just like that, you're back in the game.

All good things must come to an end, including conversations. Exiting a chat gracefully is just as necessary as starting one. You want to leave on a high note, making sure the other person feels good about the interaction. Summarize a part of the conversation to show you were paying attention: "I loved hearing about your trip to Spain; it sounds like it was an amazing experience!" Then, part with some polite and positive words, like "It was great chatting with you! Let's catch up again soon." This not only ends the conversation smoothly but also sets the stage for future interactions.

Mastering the art of conversation is like learning to dance. At first, you might step on a few toes or feel a bit clumsy. Still, with practice, you'll be twirling through dialogues at social gatherings, school events, or even in everyday chats. It's about being present, being genuine, and, most importantly, being yourself. With these tools in your communication toolkit, you're ready to turn every conversation into an opportunity to connect, impress, and express yourself. So go ahead and step into your next social interaction with confidence—the floor is yours!

Journal Prompt: The Art of Conversation

Reflect on a recent conversation in which you struggled to keep the dialogue going or felt nervous starting it. Using the tips from this section, how could you have initiated the conversation differently? What open-ended questions might you have asked to keep the conversation flowing? Also, think about a time when you handled an awkward silence or exited a conversation gracefully. Write about what you did and how it made you feel. How can you apply these strategies to future conversations to make you feel more confident and engaged?

_____

_____

_____

_____

_____

DAY 9 LISTENING SKILLS: HEARING BEYOND WORDS

So, you've nailed starting a conversation and keeping it bouncing back and forth like a good game of ping pong, but how about your listening game? Is it as sharp as your chatting skills? Listening sounds simple—just stay quiet and let the other person do the talking, right? But authentic listening, the kind that builds strong connections, is more like decoding a secret message rather than just nodding along. It's about actively engaging with what the other person is saying and showing that you really get them. Let's unpack some killer listening techniques that can turn you into the listener everyone wants to chat with.

Active listening is all about showing that you're fully tuned in and deeply engaged. It's not just about hearing words; it's about connecting. Start with your body language: nod occasionally to show you're following along, make eye contact, and maintain a posture that says, "I'm all ears!" It's like your body says, "Go on, I'm with you." Now, reflect back on what's being said. This doesn't mean you echo every word, but a quick, "So, you felt really excited when you achieved that?" shows that you're not only listening but also processing their words. This kind of feedback can make all the difference in how valued and understood someone feels during a conversation.

Now, onto the traps we all fall into sometimes. Top of the list? Interrupting. Sure, it's tempting to jump in with your own story or an opinion, but cutting someone off mid-sentence can make them feel like you're more interested in hearing your own voice than theirs. Another pitfall is preparing your response while the other person is still talking. It's like your brain is so busy drafting the next presidential speech that it forgets to listen. This can lead to missing key details, making the conversation feel disjointed. And let's not forget the big one: showing disinterest. Whether it's glancing at your phone or looking over your shoulder, these actions shout, "I'm not really interested in what you're saying," louder than words.

Listening isn't just about what is said; it's also about catching what isn't said—the pauses, the sighs, the shift in tone. These non-verbal cues can tell you heaps about what the other person is really feeling. For instance, pausing after mentioning a test might suggest they're anxious about it, even if they're playing it cool. A quick change in pitch might reveal excitement or irritation that they're not openly expressing. Tuning into these subtleties can give you deeper insight into the person's emotions and thoughts, allowing you to respond more empathetically and appropriately.

Lastly, let's talk about sealing the deal in active listening. Providing feedback that confirms understanding can significantly enhance the quality of your interactions. Summarize or paraphrase parts of the conversation to show you've been paying attention, like, "So, you're saying that you felt overlooked during the meeting?" This not only shows you're engaged but also allows the other person to clarify if you've misunderstood anything. Asking follow-up questions also plays a role here. Questions like, "What happened next?" or "How did that make you feel?" show that you're interested in digging deeper and understanding the whole picture.

By stepping up your listening game with these techniques, you're not just being polite but opening doors to deeper relationships and more meaningful connections. Whether it's with friends, family, or even teachers, showing that you genuinely listen can make you the person everyone wants to talk to. So, next time you're in a chat, put these skills to the test. Dive into the art of listening, not just to respond but to understand and connect on a whole new level.

Quiz: Listening Skills - Hearing Beyond Words

1. What is the primary goal of active listening?
    a. Nodding like a bobblehead
    b. Connecting deeply and showing understanding
    c. Preparing your next joke while they talk
2. Which of these is a sign of active listening?
    a. Staring off into space
    b. Nodding, maintaining eye contact, and reflecting back what's said
    c. Constantly checking your phone
3. What should you avoid doing to be a good listener?
    a. Interrupting with your own stories
    b. Smiling and nodding
    c. Asking follow-up questions

4. How can you show that you're interested in what the other person is saying?
   a. Glancing around the room
   b. Reflecting back their words and asking follow-up questions
   c. Saying "uh-huh" repeatedly without really paying attention

5. Which of these actions can make someone feel like you're not interested in their words?
   a. Leaning in and nodding
   b. Glancing at your phone or looking over your shoulder
   c. Maintaining eye contact and summarizing their points

6. What's a good way to handle a pause or a sigh during a conversation?
   a. Ignore it and keep talking
   b. Ask if there's something on their mind or how they're feeling
   c. Change the subject immediately

7. Why is reading between the lines in a conversation important?
   a. To pass time until it's your turn to talk
   b. To understand the speaker's emotions and respond empathetically
   c. To impress them with your mind-reading skills

Answer Key:

1. b) Connecting deeply and showing understanding
2. b) Nodding, maintaining eye contact, and reflecting back on what's said
3. a) Interrupting with your own stories

4. b) Reflecting back their words and asking follow-up questions
5. b) Glancing at your phone or looking over your shoulder
6. b) Ask if there's something on their mind or how they're feeling
7. b) To understand the speaker's emotions and respond empathetically

∾

DAY 10 BODY LANGUAGE BASICS: WHAT YOU SAY WITHOUT SPEAKING

Do you know the feeling of walking into a room and feeling like someone was upset, even though they hadn't said a word? Or maybe you've seen someone try to hide their excitement, but their wide eyes and quick movements gave it all away. That's the power of body language—it speaks volumes without making a sound. Whether you realize it or not, the way you sit, stand, smile, or frown can communicate just as much as any words that come out of your mouth. Mastering the art of body language can dramatically transform your ability to communicate effectively. So, let's break down what your body could be telling other people and how you can make sure it's saying what you actually mean.

First off, non-verbal cues include all the ways you communicate without words. This encompasses facial expressions, gestures, posture, and even how much space you take up. For instance, think about what a furrowed brow and crossed arms suggest compared to a smile and open hands. The first combo screams, "Back off!" while the second one is practically an invitation to chat. Being aware of these cues in yourself and others can help you read a room better and adapt your behavior to better fit the situation. It's like having a secret insight into what everyone is really thinking, which can be super helpful in navigating social interactions, from tense group projects to chill hangouts.

Now, onto crafting the right signals. Positive body language, like smiling and an open posture, can make you seem approachable and friendly. Smiling not only makes you more attractive but also emits enthusiasm, making others feel more comfortable around you. An open posture—like not crossing your arms or legs—suggests you're open to communication and willing to engage. Mirroring, or subtly copying someone else's body language, is another powerful tool. If they lean in, you lean in; if they lower their voice, you do the same. This can create a feeling of empathy and understanding, showing that you are engaged and in tune with how they are feeling.

On the flip side, certain types of body language can throw up barriers. Crossed arms can make you appear defensive or closed off, even if you're just cold or trying to get comfortable. Avoiding eye contact might make you seem disinterested or, worse, like you have something to hide. And let's not forget fidgeting, which can signal nervousness or impatience. While it's totally normal to feel anxious or restless, unchecked fidgeting can be distracting and might make others feel uneasy. Being conscious of these signals and adjusting your body language can help prevent miscommunications and make your interactions smoother and more positive.

Finally, it's imperative to align your verbal and non-verbal cues. Have you ever told someone you were fine when you were clearly upset? Your words said one thing, but your body likely told the truth. When your body language doesn't match your words, it can confuse the listener and make you seem untrustworthy or insincere. Striving for consistency between what you say and how you say it helps reinforce your message and builds trust with others. If you're excited about something, let your whole body show it. If you're apologizing, make sure your posture and expressions convey sincerity. This alignment not only helps others understand you better but also boosts your confidence in your communication skills.

By becoming more aware of your body language and the signals you're sending, you can take your communication skills to a whole new level. It's not just about using your words wisely; it's about making your entire body talk the talk. Whether you're aiming to make new friends, ace a job interview, or just get through a family dinner, paying attention to the unspoken dialogue can make all the difference. So, next time you find yourself in a social setting, take a moment to assess not just what you're saying but how you're saying it—all without saying a word.

Quiz: Body Language Basics - What You Say Without Speaking

1. What is body language?
    a. The way you dance like nobody's watching
    b. Non-verbal cues like facial expressions, gestures, and posture
    c. Using interpretive dance to communicate
2. What do a furrowed brow and crossed arms typically suggest?
    a. You're trying to become a human pretzel
    b. Defensiveness or frustration
    c. You're just really cold and need a hug

3. Which of the following is an example of positive body language?
   a. Smiling and having an open posture
   b. Pretending to be a statue
   c. Tapping your foot like you're in a drum solo
4. How can mirroring someone's body language help in a conversation?
   a. It makes you look like a synchronized swimmer
   b. It creates a sense of empathy and understanding
   c. It confuses the other person into thinking you're their twin
5. What should you avoid doing to prevent sending negative body language signals?
   a. Crossing your arms and turning into a human pretzel
   b. Maintaining eye contact like you're in a staring contest
   c. Nodding so much you look like a bobblehead
6. Why is it essential to align your verbal and non-verbal cues?
   a. To create a secret dance language
   b. To make you seem like a mind reader
   c. To reinforce your message and build trust

Answer Key:

1. b) Non-verbal cues like facial expressions, gestures, and posture
2. b) Defensiveness or frustration
3. a) Smiling and having an open posture
4. b) It creates a sense of empathy and understanding
5. a) Crossing your arms and turning into a human pretzel
6. c) To reinforce your message and build trust

~

DAY 11 ASSERTIVENESS TRAINING: EXPRESS YOURSELF WITHOUT FEAR

Let's talk about assertiveness, not to be confused with its distant cousins, aggression and passivity. Imagine assertiveness as the Goldilocks of communication styles—it's just right. It's about being upfront about your needs and feelings without stepping on anyone else's toes. This isn't about transforming you into a debate champ who dominates every conversation, nor is it about making you a wallflower who only nods and smiles. Assertiveness is about finding that sweet spot where your voice is heard just as loudly as everyone else's.

So, what exactly is assertiveness? It's the ability to express your thoughts, feelings, and beliefs in an open, honest, and direct way while still respecting others. It's not about being pushy (that's aggression) or mumbling your opinion and hoping someone hears (that's passiveness). Assertiveness is your communication backbone; it lets you stand up for yourself without knocking others down. This skill is crucial not just in dodging peer pressure or handling a disagreement but also in everyday interactions, like choosing a movie with friends or discussing a poor grade with a teacher. It's about being respectful yet firm, clear yet courteous.

Now, how do you actually communicate assertively? Enter "I" statements, a game-changer in the world of communication. Instead of saying, "You make me so mad," which sounds pretty confrontational and might put the other person in defensive mode, try, "I feel upset when you interrupt me because I think what I have to say matters too." See the twist? This approach focuses on your feelings and perceptions without blaming or accusing the other person. It's like saying, "Here's what's up with me," without adding, "...and it's all your fault." Using "I" statements helps keep the conversation calm and focused and opens the door for productive, respectful dialogue.

Conflicts are like vegetables—nobody's favorite part of the meal but inevitable and good for you if handled right. Assertiveness shines brightest in these tricky situations. It's about expressing your viewpoint clearly and respectfully while also being open to hearing the other side. Say you're in a group project, and two members have conflicting ideas. Instead of picking sides or avoiding the tension, you could steer the conversation with, "I see both points have their merits. How about we find a compromise that incorporates both ideas?" This approach not only diffuses tension but also shows that you value both perspectives. It's about navigating the conflict, not escalating it.

Journal Prompt: Assertiveness Training: Express Yourself without Fear

> Reflect on a recent situation where you felt you weren't able to express your thoughts or feelings openly. How did it make you feel, and what was the outcome? Using the techniques discussed in this section, think about how you could have approached the situation more assertively. Write down an "I" statement you could have used to express yourself clearly and respectfully. For example, "I feel frustrated when our gatherings run late because it affects my ability to complete other tasks." How do you think using

assertiveness might have changed the outcome?

_____

_____

_____

_____

_____

DAY 12 THE POWER OF EMPATHY: CONNECTING ON A DEEPER LEVEL

Imagine you're watching one of those movies where the main character feels what everyone else is feeling. Sounds exhausting, right? But also, imagine how understanding they are in their relationships. That's empathy in a nutshell—not so much feeling everyone's emotional baggage but understanding and sharing their feelings as if they were your own. Empathy is like a super glue for human connections; it's what helps us bond and understand each other on a deeper level. And when it comes to talking and listening, empathy turns ordinary exchanges into meaningful conversations.

So, what exactly is empathy? It's the ability to put yourself in someone else's shoes—to understand their feelings and perspectives without judgment. It's seeing the world through their eyes and connecting with their emotions. Why is this important? Because empathy breeds compassion and trust, the foundations of any strong relationship. Whether it's with friends, family, or even acquaintances, empathy allows you to navigate social interactions more smoothly, making others feel valued and understood. It's a crucial skill in building bridges and healing wounds, not just in personal relationships but also in broader social contexts.

Empathetic listening is about more than just hearing words; it's about tuning into the emotions behind them. Imagine a friend telling you about a rough day at school. Instead of just nodding and thinking about what to say next, empathetic listening involves really hearing their frustration and disappointment. You might reflect this understanding back to them by saying, "That sounds really tough. It must have been frustrating to deal with that." This kind of response not only shows that you are listening but that you also care about their feelings. Techniques like mirroring their emotions or summarizing what they've said are great ways to practice empathetic listening. It's about making the speaker feel seen and understood, which can significantly deepen the connection between you.

But empathy isn't just about listening; it's also about how you respond. Expressing empathy can transform a simple conversation into a bridge of deeper understanding. It involves more than just understanding someone's emotions —it's about validating them and showing genuine concern. For instance, if someone is excited about a new project, express your excitement with them. Say something like, "That sounds amazing! You must be thrilled!" This kind of empathetic response not only acknowledges their feelings but also shares in their emotional experience, creating a shared moment of joy.

Empathy really shows its strength in sensitive or difficult situations. For example, suppose you're in a heated debate. In that case, trying to see the other person's point of view can help de-escalate the situation. It allows you to address conflicts with a cooler head and a warmer heart. Even in everyday interactions, empathy can smooth over potential bumps. It helps you understand where the other person is coming from, which can prevent misunderstandings and build a more supportive environment. Whether you're consoling a friend who's going through a tough time or trying to understand a parent's perspective on curfews, empathy can open doors to more effective and compassionate communication.

By weaving empathy into your conversations, you're not just talking; you're connecting on a human level. This doesn't mean you have to agree with everyone all the time or take on everyone's emotional baggage. It's about acknowledging their feelings as valid and trying to understand their perspective. This can lead to more meaningful relationships and a greater sense of connection with those around you. As you continue to practice empathy, you'll find that it not only enriches your conversations but also enriches your relationships, making them stronger and more resilient.

Activity: Empathy in Action

Develop your empathetic skills through observation and reflection.

Observation Journal: Spend a day observing the interactions around you. Pay close attention to the body language, facial expressions, and tones of voice of people you encounter. Note down specific instances where you think someone is expressing a strong emotion, like happiness, frustration, or sadness.

Reflect on Feelings: In your journal, write a short reflection for each instance you observed. Try to describe what the person might be feeling and why. For example, "I noticed my friend seemed quiet and with-drawn during lunch. They might be feeling overwhelmed or sad because they have a lot of schoolwork."

Empathy Mapping: Choose one of the instances you observed and create an empathy map. Divide a piece of paper into four sections labeled "Says," "Thinks," "Does," and "Feels." Fill in each section with what you think the person was expressing verbally ("Says"), what they might be thinking ("Thinks"), their actions ("Does"), and their emotions ("Feels").

Action Plan: Think about how you could respond empathetically in one of the situations you observed. Write down a few sentences of what you might say to show empathy. For example, "If I notice my friend is quiet and seems sad, I might say, 'You seem a bit down today. Do you want to talk about what's bothering you?'"

Practice Empathetic Responses: Over the next few days, try to apply your action plan in real interactions. Observe the responses you get and how they change the dynamics of your conversations. Note any positive changes or challenges you encounter.

Example Observation and Reflection:

Observation: I saw my classmate, Charlie, looking stressed before our math test. He was pacing and frowning.

Reflection: Charlie might be feeling anxious about the test because he mentioned he didn't have much time to study.

Empathy Map:
- Says: "I didn't get much time to study."
- Thinks: "I'm worried I won't do well."
- Does: Pacing, frowning.
- Feels: Anxious, stressed.

Action Plan: "Hey Charlie, I noticed you seem a bit stressed about the test. Do you want to go over some main points together before it starts?"

As we wrap up this section on mastering communication skills, remember that each skill—whether it's starting conversations, listening actively, understanding body language, asserting yourself, or practicing empathy—plays a vital role in enhancing your ability to connect with others. These skills go beyond mere communication tools; they serve as pathways to a richer understanding and more fulfilling connections. Continue to refine these abilities, and you'll see a remarkable transformation in your social interactions, making each conversation a step toward stronger and more meaningful relationships. Up next, we'll dive into navigating digital social spaces, where communication takes on new challenges and opportunities in the digital age.

With each new branch, the tree extends its reach, much like
mastering communication. It learns to spread its influence and
connect with others, creating a network that supports its
continued growth and vitality.

SECTION 4 NAVIGATING DIGITAL SOCIAL SPACES

"Be yourself; everyone else is already taken"

OSCAR WILDE

I magine your online persona as a digital superhero version of you. Now, what if I told you that sometimes, without even noticing, we might be creating a persona that's a bit too over-the-top or polishing an image that's just a little too perfect? Navigating the social media universe requires more than just flashy posts; it's about crafting an online identity that indeed echoes who you are, not just who you think you should be. Let's dive into the art of staying authentic online, dodging the pitfalls of a fabricated image, and keeping it real across different platforms.

~

DAY 13 MANAGING YOUR ONLINE PERSONA: STAYING TRUE ONLINE

Creating and maintaining an online persona that genuinely reflects your true self and values isn't just about avoiding a few fibs about your weekend activities. It's about aligning your digital expressions with your real-world self. Think about the aspects of your personality you're proud of—maybe it's your quirky sense of humor, your passion for art, or your advocacy for mental health. These are the gems to highlight in your online persona. But here's the kicker: authenticity. It's the secret ingredient that makes your digital self resonate with others. When you share real experiences, genuine thoughts, and true feelings, you create deeper connections than any filter could ever manufacture. So next time you post, ask yourself, "Is this me, or is it just what I think looks cool?"

Now, let's talk about the flip side: the risks of rocking a more fake than a true persona. Crafting an image that's far removed from who you really are can lead to a host of troubles, like the classic case of trust issues. Suppose your friends or followers discover the disconnect between your online persona and your actual life. In that case, their trust can evaporate faster than a Snap story. Beyond that, maintaining a false front is like wearing a mask that's too tight—it's uncomfortable, and you can't keep it on forever without slipping. Plus, the stress of upholding a fabricated image can really weigh you down. Why choose that when being your genuine self is so much lighter?

Keeping your online persona consistent across different platforms is like making sure your story stays the same whether you're on Instagram, TikTok, or Snapchat. It doesn't mean you can't tailor your content to fit the vibe of each platform

—go ahead and get artsy on Insta and goofy on TikTok—but the core, the real you, should remain unchanged. Consistency helps you build a coherent brand for yourself, one that's easily recognizable and reliably genuine. It's about making sure that whether someone scrolls through your TikTok dances or your Insta stories, they're getting the same authentic slice of your life.

Let's bring in some real-life flavor. Consider Jamie, who once juggled multiple online personas—one for each social media platform. Instagram Jamie was an adventurer climbing mountains every weekend (even though he actually just climbed the stairs to his apartment), while on Twitter, Jamie was a hot-take artist on all things political (despite not being able to vote yet). It was exhausting and confusing. Eventually, Jamie decided to simplify his digital life, aligning his online presence with his real interests—comic books and coding. The result? He had deeper connections with followers who shared his genuine passions and a lot less stress about keeping up false pretenses.

Or take Peyton, who initially hid her love for anime on social media because she thought it was "too nerdy." When she finally started sharing her artwork inspired by her favorite shows, she was overwhelmed by the positive response. She discovered a community of fans just like her. This authenticity brought her not only closer friendships but also opportunities to collaborate with other artists and creators. By embracing her true self, Peyton turned her social media into a portal of opportunities and genuine interactions.

Navigating your digital social spaces with authenticity and consistency isn't just about crafting a likable online persona; it's about creating a space where you can connect truthfully and freely. It's about letting your digital footprint be a true reflection of your footsteps in the real world. So, next time you log in, remember that the best character you can play online is yourself.

Quiz: Managing Your Online Persona - Staying True Online

1. What's the secret ingredient to making your digital self resonate with others?
   a. Posting only pictures of your pet rock
   b. Authenticity
   c. Pretending to be a time-traveling wizard
2. What can happen if your online persona is more fake than true?
   a. Your friends will think you're a secret superhero
   b. You might face trust issues and feel like a stressed-out pineapple
   c. You'll gain the ability to speak fluent dolphin
3. How can you keep your online persona consistent across different platforms?
   a. By posting cat memes exclusively
   b. By staying true to your core self while tailoring content to fit each platform's vibe
   c. By using the same filter that makes you look like a space alien
4. What lesson did Jamie learn from juggling multiple online personas?
   a. It's fun to have different personas everywhere, like being a secret agent
   b. Simplifying his digital life and being genuine led to deeper connections and less stress
   c. It's easy to confuse everyone and make them think you're a shape-shifter

5. How did Peyton benefit from sharing her true interests online?
   a. She discovered she's actually a wizard in disguise
   b. She found a community of fans, made closer friendships, and got new opportunities
   c. She had to join a secret society of anime enthusiasts

Answer Key:

1. b) Authenticity
2. b) You might face trust issues and feel like a stressed-out pineapple
3. b) By staying true to your core self while tailoring content to fit each platform's vibe
4. b) Simplifying his digital life and being genuine led to deeper connections and less stress
5. b) She found a community of fans, made closer friendships, and got new opportunities

~

DAY 14 CYBERBULLYING: DEALING WITH DIGITAL HARASSMENT

Let's tackle a challenging but essential topic—cyberbullying. Imagine you're just chilling, scrolling through your feed, and then, bam, you find nasty comments or direct messages aimed at tearing you down. Not cool, right? Cyberbullying is like the villain of the digital world, lurking behind screens and sowing negativity. It's more than just a disagreement or a one-off rude comment; it's a repeated pattern meant to intimidate, embarrass, or insult. Think of texts, posts, tweets, or memes that keep targeting someone to make them feel small or scared. This digital menace can sneak up in many forms, whether it's spreading rumors, sharing embarrassing photos without consent, or hurling insults. Understanding what qualifies as cyberbullying is the first step in fighting back.

Now, how do you deal with these digital bullies? First up, know when to pick your battles. If it's just a random mean comment, sometimes the best response is no response. Ignoring the bait can often make trolls lose interest. But what if it doesn't stop? Or what if the comments are seriously harmful? That's when you step up your game. Respond, but keep it classy and calm. A simple "Please stop; your comments are hurtful" might do the trick. However, if the harassment escalates, it's time to bring in reinforcements—report the behavior to the platform and talk to someone you trust, like a parent or teacher. They can help you take further action, like contacting the cyberbully's parents or even the authorities if things get really serious.

Preventing cyberbullying starts with guarding your digital gates. Tighten up your privacy settings so only people you trust can see your posts or send you messages. Think of it as setting up a sound security system in your digital house. Also, be mindful of who you connect with online. Not everyone who sends a friend request or follows you need to be let into your virtual space. It's okay to be selective; after all, your online wellbeing is at stake.

Support is paramount when dealing with cyberbullying. Remember, you're not alone in this. Websites like StopBullying.gov provide resources and advice on handling cyberbullying effectively. Many social media platforms have guidelines and tools for reporting abusive content and behavior, making it easier to take action against bullies.

Schools often have policies and counselors who can offer support and intervene if necessary. Knowing these resources can empower you to stand up against cyberbullies with confidence.

Navigating the digital world can sometimes feel like walking through a minefield, but understanding the ins and outs of cyberbullying, knowing how to respond, and taking preventive measures can make you a savvy and safe digital citizen. Equip yourself with knowledge, and don't hesitate to seek help when needed. Your online space should be a place of positivity and self-expression, not fear or negativity. So, keep these tips in your back pocket and surf the web boldly and wisely.

Journal Prompt: Cyberbullying: Dealing with Digital Harassment

Reflect on a time when you or someone you know experienced negative behavior online. How did it make you feel, and what steps did you take to address it? If you could go back, what would you do differently using the tips mentioned in this section? Write about how you can strengthen your online privacy and support systems to protect yourself and others from cyberbullying better. How can you contribute to creating a more positive and supportive digital community?

DAY 15 SOCIAL MEDIA BALANCE: ONLINE AND OFFLINE LIFE

Let's face it: the digital world has its perks, but sometimes, it feels like we're all starring in a movie where smartphones are glued to our hands—plot twist, it's actually reality! While scrolling through feeds and snapping pics can be loads of fun, it's vital to catch the signs when social media starts playing the villain in your real life. Maybe you've noticed that your legs feel as stiff as a pair of jeans left out in the cold because your daily walks have turned into scrolling marathons. Or perhaps real conversations have become as rare as an unfiltered selfie, and your sleep schedule is as erratic as a cat in a laser pointer factory. These are the flashing neon signs that social media might be steering your life a bit off course.

Recognizing these red flags is the first step. The next is setting boundaries—because managing your social media isn't about cutting it out of your life; it's about ensuring it doesn't overshadow everything else. Think about creating specific hours for when you dive into the digital world. Maybe decide that meal times are phone-free or that after 9 p.m., your phone gets as much sleep as you do. Establishing tech-free zones or periods can also work wonders. Perhaps make your bedroom a sanctuary where phones fear to tread or keep the dinner table a place for face-to-face chats instead of digital distractions. It's about creating pockets of peace where real life gets the spotlight, not just the screen glare.

Now, let's chat about the unsung heroes of your story— offline activities. Remember the simple joys of shooting hoops, diving into the pages of a gripping novel, or hiking through nature? These activities aren't just fun; they're like personal trainers for your wellbeing. Engaging in sports can boost your physical health and teach teamwork while losing yourself in a book enhances empathy and reduces stress. And let's not forget the magic of being in nature; it's like hitting the refresh button on your soul. Each of these activities offers a unique blend of benefits that help you grow stronger, smarter, and more connected to the world around you. They remind you that a big, beautiful offline world is waiting to be explored—a world where experiences are felt, not just filtered.

Balancing online and offline life is truly an art form in today's digital age. It's about weaving through your day with the awareness to know when to log in and when to log off. Imagine managing your time like a DJ mixes tracks. Sometimes, you're tuned into the digital beat; other times, you're grooving to the live vibes of the world around you. It's about finding that rhythm that keeps your social life enriched and varied, ensuring that your digital interactions are just part of a larger, vibrant social dance. So, as you navigate this connected world, keep tuning into the cues of your own needs and make sure that your tech habits don't drown out the beautiful complexities of face-to-face connections and real-world adventures. Keep the balance, and you'll not only enhance your social skills but enrich your life with a diversity of experiences that no online platform can replicate.

Activity: Balancing Online and Offline Life

Self-Assessment: Spend a day noting how much time you spend on social media and other online activities. Use a journal or a time-tracking app to record your usage.

Identify Red Flags: Reflect on your notes and identify any red flags such as feeling stiff from sitting too long, missing out on in-person interactions, or disrupted sleep patterns.

Set Boundaries: Choose at least two boundaries to implement. Here are some examples:

- Designate tech-free times (for example, no phone use after 9 p.m. or during meals).

- Create tech-free zones (for example, no phones in the bedroom or at the dinner table).

Explore Offline Activities: Make a list of three offline activities you enjoy or would like to try. Examples include playing a sport, reading a book, going for a hike, or practicing a hobby like drawing or playing an instrument. Schedule time for these activities in your weekly agenda or task tracker.

Tech-Free Challenge: Choose one day in the next week to take the "Tech-Free Challenge." Commit to spending at least half the day without any social media or unnecessary online activity. Use this time to engage in the offline activities you listed.

Reflection: At the end of the week, reflect on your experience. Write about how the tech-free time made you feel. Did you notice any changes in your mood, focus, or relationships? Were there any challenges? How can you continue to balance your online and offline life moving forward?

Example Schedule:

Social Media Challenge
7-Day Challenge

Monday - Track social media usage. Identify red flags.

Tuesday - Set boundaries (e.g., no phone use during dinner). List offline activities.

Wednesday - schedule offline activities.

Thursday - Begin implementing tech-free times.

Friday - Continue implementing tech-free times.

Saturday - Tech-Free Challenge Day.

Sunday - Reflect on the week and plan for ongoing balance.

DAY 16 DIGITAL ETIQUETTE: RULES OF ONLINE ENGAGEMENT

Navigating the digital world is a lot like attending a giant, never-ending party. Everyone's invited, and while it's buzzing with exciting conversations, it's also a place where manners matter. That's where digital etiquette comes into play—it's the rulebook for behaving properly online. Think of it as the unwritten code that helps keep interactions respectful and constructive. Understanding digital etiquette starts with some basics: think before you post, respect others' opinions, and be mindful of the impact your words and images can have. It's easy to forget that behind every profile picture and username is a real person with real feelings. So, before hitting that post or comment button, take a moment to consider how your words could affect them.

One of the biggest social mistakes in the digital world is oversharing. Sure, it's tempting to share every detail of your life online, from your breakfast burrito to your late-night thoughts about the universe. But remember, the internet never forgets. Oversharing can not only bore your audience but also expose you to risks like identity theft or just plain embarrassment. Another common mistake is posting sensitive content without thinking. Whether it's a heated opinion post or a photo from that wild party last weekend, ask yourself if it's something you'd be comfortable with everyone seeing—from your best friend to your grandma to a future employer.

Engaging in online arguments can also be a slippery slope. The anonymity of the internet can lead some to say things they would never say face-to-face, turning what could be a healthy debate into an all-out war. If you find yourself in a heated discussion, take a deep breath and strive for a polite and respectful tone. Remember, winning an argument isn't worth losing a friend or sullying your online reputation.

Now, let's talk about how to keep your digital interactions positive. Using polite language goes a long way. Simple phrases like "please" and "thank you" can soften requests and show gratitude, making others more receptive to your messages. Being inclusive is also important. The internet is a global village, full of diverse cultures, viewpoints, and backgrounds. Embracing this diversity not only enriches your online experience but also promotes a sense of community and respect.

Disagreeing respectfully is perhaps one of the most valuable skills in digital etiquette. It's perfectly fine to have different opinions, but the way you express these differences can either bridge gaps or widen them. Instead of attacking someone's viewpoint, try to understand where they're coming from and explain your perspective in a way that's open and low-key. A little compassion can turn a potential conflict into an opportunity for mutual understanding.

To bring these points to life, consider the scenario of responding to a provocative message. Imagine someone posts a comment on your video that you find offensive. Your first impulse might be to fire back with something equally harsh, but that only adds fuel to the fire. A more effective approach would be to either ignore the comment, if it's openly trolling, or respond calmly, clarifying why you find the comment inappropriate and inviting the person to a more constructive conversation. This not only maintains your dignity but also sets a positive tone for others who might read the exchange.

In another scenario, if you see someone being harassed online, stepping in can be tricky but essential. A supportive comment showing solidarity with the person being targeted can discourage the harasser and empower the victim. You might also privately message the person being harassed to offer your support and encourage them to report the harassment if it continues.

Navigating the digital landscape with proper etiquette isn't just about avoiding missteps; it's about actively creating a positive, respectful online environment. By thinking before you post, respecting diverse opinions, and engaging constructively, you help set the tone for your digital circles. Just like in real life, a little courtesy goes a long way online. Whether you're commenting on a friend's post, debating in a forum, or sharing your latest photos, how you conduct yourself can make all the difference. So, the next time you log on, remember that your words and actions contribute to the vibe of the vast digital party. Make it a good one!

Journal Prompt: Digital Etiquette: Rules of Online Engagement

Reflect on a recent online interaction. Did you handle it well, or could you have responded better? Consider these questions:
- What was the situation, and how did you respond?
- Did you follow digital etiquette rules like thinking before posting, using polite language, or respecting opinions?
- How did your actions affect the other person and the conversation?
- What will you do differently next time to ensure a positive interaction?
Write a brief plan for incorporating good

digital etiquette into your daily online
activities.

_____

_____

_____

_____

_____

KEEPING CONVERSATIONS POSITIVE AND PRODUCTIVE

In the digital realm, similar to a video game, you'll have fun
moments and make dope connections. Still, you'll also have
to deal with things like avoiding negativity and how you
handle your online interactions, from DMs to comments,
which shape not just your online rep but also how you
interact with people in real life. Let's level up your digital
communication skills to keep things respectful, avoid drama,
handle disagreements smoothly, and stay positive.

Digital communication etiquette mirrors the courtesy we
apply in real life, and it has changed for the online world. It's
about being clear, respectful, and kind. Before sending a
message, consider if you would say it face-to-face. This
reflection encourages kindness and transparency, reducing

the chance of misunderstanding. In digital spaces where tone can be unclear, choose words that foster positive interactions, steering clear of sarcasm and slang that could confuse your global audience.

The absence of non-verbal cues online makes it easy for messages to be misunderstood. To prevent this, provide context for your jokes or sarcasm with a simple "lol" or emoji and elaborate on more serious topics to ensure clarity. If misunderstandings occur, address them swiftly with a clarification to prevent things from getting out of hand. Clear communication minimizes confusion and maintains smooth digital interactions.

Online disagreements can get heated fast without the benefit of face-to-face interaction. When things start to get tense, take a moment to pause and think before you reply. Focus on what's being said, not who's saying it, and try to use facts and logic instead of getting aggressive. If the argument isn't going anywhere, stepping back and agreeing to disagree is okay. That way, you can keep the conversation chill and productive.

Aim to be a force of positivity in your online communities. Share uplifting content, engage positively in discussions, and offer support. Small acts of kindness, like complimenting a post or sharing helpful resources, can have a significant impact, enabling a supportive digital environment. By making it a priority to provide clear, respectful communication, you'll not only improve your online interactions but also contribute to a healthier digital community. Your next post or comment could spark a new friendship, hobby, or even future opportunity. Practice strong digital manners to improve your online world.

PRIVACY PROTECTIONS: SAFEGUARDING YOUR DIGITAL FOOTPRINT

Your digital footprint—comprising tweets, shares, and online activities—follows you everywhere in the digital realm. Unlike a shadow, it can cause trouble if not managed wisely. Online privacy means having control over your personal information, such as your name, birthday, and browsing habits. Each time you engage online by signing up for apps, posting on social media, or visiting websites, your information is collected, which could lead to identity theft or unwanted attention if mishandled. Knowing what information you're sharing and with whom matters.

Think of online privacy as a defense strategy. Begin by familiarizing yourself with the privacy settings on social media platforms like Instagram, Facebook, and TikTok, adjusting them to control who sees and interacts with your posts. Be mindful about sharing location details and personal information like your home address or school name. Limiting this sharing can protect you from potential risks.

Privacy breaches can have serious consequences, ranging from identity theft to cyberstalking, impacting both your digital and real-life well-being. Such incidents can lead to unauthorized charges on credit cards or unwelcome personal attacks, highlighting the importance of active privacy management.

Regularly reviewing your privacy settings, much like checking game stats or homework, can prevent privacy mishaps. Apps and platforms update their policies frequently, so stay informed to protect your digital presence effectively. Treat these check-ups as essential upkeep for your online health. Navigating online privacy can be challenging, but with the proper knowledge and actions, you can maintain a clean digital footprint and safeguard your personal information. As you engage online, remember to manage your digital interactions with the same care and respect as those in real life, ensuring a respectful and protected digital existence. Moving forward, we'll explore personal growth and self-discovery, emphasizing the development of your identity and values in both the online and offline worlds.

As the tree blossoms, its flowers represent the blooming of connections in digital spaces. Each flower, a new opportunity, symbolizes the diverse and vibrant interactions that help the tree—and the individual—flourish in an ever-connected world.

SECTION 5 EMBRACING INDIVIDUALITY AND AUTHENTICITY

"Why fit in when you were born to stand out?"

DR. SEUSS

Do you know what it's like when you're on an endless quest, like a character in an epic video game, trying to unlock the secret level where you finally figure out what you're genuinely passionate about? Well, spoiler alert: discovering what makes you tick isn't about stumbling upon a hidden treasure. It's more like crafting your own map as you go, marking spots of joy and intrigue. This section is your DIY kit for crafting that map and exploring territories of interest that make you, well, you! So, let's roll up our sleeves and dig into the exciting world of passions and how they weave into the fabric of your well-being.

~

DAY 17 DISCOVERING YOUR PASSIONS: EXPLORING WHAT MAKES YOU TICK

First off, let's deal with the big question: "How do I figure out what I'm passionate about?" Think about the last time you completely lost track of time doing something. Maybe you were sketching, coding a new app, or experimenting with recipes in the kitchen—activities where the world seemed to fade away, and it was just you and your craft. These are clues.

To start this exploration, grab a journal or open a new digital doc and list activities that absorb you completely. Don't judge or censor your interests; just jot them down. This list is your personal interest inventory, the raw materials we'll use to map out your passion project.

Now, with your list in hand, it's time to play mad scientist with your interests. Experimentation is vital to transforming vague interests into full-blown passions. Choose one interest from your list and dive deeper. Sign up for a workshop, join a club, or set up a personal project related to it. The goal here isn't to immediately excel but to explore. You might discover a hidden talent or realize that something isn't quite as exciting as you thought—and that's totally fine. Each experiment brings you closer to understanding what truly fires you up. Remember, Edison didn't invent the lightbulb on his first try; it took lots of attempts and learning from each failure. Approach each new activity with curiosity and resilience. Who knows? Your next try might light up your world.

While we're on this exploratory trail, let's talk about why following your passions isn't just fun but also essential for your mental and emotional health. Engaging in activities that you love can dramatically boost your mood and self-esteem. It gives you a sense of purpose and accomplishment, like adding a rare achievement badge to your life's gaming profile. For instance, consider the story of Alex, a teen who discovered a passion for photography. Through his lens, he found a new way to connect with the world, capturing moments that often went unnoticed. His anxiety, which frequently made school a challenge, found a quiet space among the clicks of his camera. This isn't just about filling time; it's about enriching your life's portfolio with experiences that resonate with your soul.

Finally, let's ensure these newfound or deepening interests don't just end up as weekend hobbies. Integrating your passions into daily life can enhance your everyday happiness and self-discovery journey. Start small; maybe it's reading a page of a novel each night, sketching during lunch, or coding for thirty minutes in the morning. Think of these activities not as additional tasks on your to-do list but as non-negotiable appointments with joy. They are as important as your daily meals—a nourishment for your spirit.

As you map out your passions and experiment with new activities, remember that this process is uniquely yours. It's about finding what makes your heart race a bit faster, your mind engage a bit deeper, and your smile stretches a bit wider. Whether it's playing guitar, coding, painting, or something entirely out of the box, each step towards recognizing and welcoming your passions is a step towards a more vibrant, authentically happy you. So keep exploring, keep experimenting, and let your passions lead you to new heights of joy and fulfillment.

Activity: Discovering Your Passions - Exploring What Makes You Tick

Interest Inventory: Spend 10 minutes listing

activities that make you lose track of time. Think about moments when you felt absorbed entirely and happy.

Choose and Explore: Pick one interest from your list to explore further this week. Research ways to dive deeper into this interest, such as online tutorials, clubs, or workshops.

Experiment: Dedicate at least 1 hour this week to experimenting with your chosen interest. Keep a journal to note what you enjoyed, what you learned, and any challenges you faced.

Reflect on Well-being: After your experiment, reflect on how engaging in this activity made you feel. Did it boost your mood? Did you feel a sense of accomplishment?

Daily Integration: Think of small ways to integrate this interest into your daily routine.

- Examples: Spend 10 minutes sketching each day or read a chapter of a book each night.

Share and Connect: Share your experience with a friend or family member. Discuss what you discovered and how you plan to continue exploring your passion.

DAY 18 VALUES AND BELIEFS: STANDING BY WHAT YOU BELIEVE IN

Imagine you're the main character in a video game, where each level tests not just your skills but your decisions based on your core beliefs. What do you stand for? What won't you stand for? These aren't just filler for your character's bio; they're the principles guiding your every move. Understanding and defining your personal values isn't just about building a moral compass—it's like programming your internal GPS to navigate life's twists and turns.

So, how do you start this quest of identifying your personal values? Think of moments that made you feel really proud or deeply satisfied. Perhaps it was a time when you stood up for a friend or completed a project that made a difference. Each of these moments is a clue to what you truly value. To get these values out of the abstract and into your daily life, try this: create a "Values Map." Grab a piece of paper, and write down stories from your life that felt significant. Next to each, note what value was at play—was it fairness, compassion, or imagination? Seeing your values spelled out helps solidify them in your mind and shows you when and how you're already living according to them.

Now, wielding your values isn't just about having them; it's about using them to steer your choices. Every decision, from how you handle a disagreement to what you post online, is a chance to align with your values. This alignment matters because it not only ensures consistency in your actions but also strengthens your sense of self. When faced with a tough choice, ask yourself: "Does this align with my values?" This question can be your north star, keeping you true to yourself even when external pressures push you towards easier or more popular paths. It's like having a secret weapon that shields you from choices that could lead you astray.

But here's the thing: everyone's values map looks different. And that's not just okay; it's necessary for a vibrant, diverse society. It is essential to learn to respect and understand where others are coming from, even if their values differ from yours. This doesn't mean you have to agree with every-one; instead, it's about acknowledging their right to their perspectives. This respect is the foundation of empathy and tolerance. It allows for healthier debates, more inclusive communities, and deeper connections. Think of it as being an ambassador in your own life, navigating through diverse value landscapes with respect and openness.

Putting your values into action can be one of the most rewarding aspects of knowing what you stand for. Whether it's through volunteering, participating in community projects, or standing up against injustices, these actions cement your values not just in your mind but in your world. Take, for example, teens who organize or participate in local clean-ups because they value environmental conservation or those who volunteer at food banks because they believe in helping those in need. Each act of service is a ripple, spreading the impact of your values across your community and beyond. Even everyday actions, like choosing to speak kindly or opting to share over competing, are ways to live out your values. These choices might seem small, but they are profound in their impact, reinforcing the type of person you choose to be every day.

As you continue to explore and define what you truly stand for, remember that your values are your anchors and guides. They are uniquely yours, and they give your actions and decisions both purpose and depth. Living in alignment with your values isn't just about making good choices; it's about making your choices suitable for you, ensuring they reflect the person you aspire to be. So keep reflecting, keep respect-ing, and keep acting in ways that speak true to the values you hold dear. This is how you craft a life that is not only successful but also significant.

Journal Prompt: Values and Beliefs: Standing by What You Believe In

Reflect on a moment when you felt incredibly proud or deeply satisfied. What happened, and what values were at play? Write about why this moment was significant to you and how it reflects your core beliefs.

Next, think about a recent decision you made. How did your values influence that decision? If you could go back, would you change anything to better align with your values?

Finally, consider how you can put your values into action in your daily life. List three actions or decisions you can make this week that align with your core beliefs. Reflect on how living in alignment with your values makes you feel and how it impacts those around you.

DAY 19 THE ART OF BEING DIFFERENT: THRIVING AS YOURSELF

Let's face it: Being a teen can sometimes feel like you're auditioning for a role in a show where everyone expects you to fit a specific role. But here's a thought: what if you tossed the script and wrote your own? Embracing your uniqueness isn't just about standing out from the crowd; it's about being comfortable in your own skin, quirks and all. Think about all the most memorable characters in your favorite shows or books; don't their unique traits make them so special? That's the power of individuality, and guess what? You've got it too.

So, how do you start celebrating what makes you different? It begins with recognizing and appreciating the qualities that set you apart. Maybe you have an eclectic style, a quirky sense of humor, or an unusual hobby. These aren't things to hide; they're your superpowers. Embracing these traits can feel like a breath of fresh air like you're finally allowing yourself just to be you. And the cool part? Celebrating your uniqueness can inspire others to embrace their own differences. It creates a ripple effect that enriches your environment, making it a more diverse and vibrant place to be. Imagine a world where everyone felt free to be themselves without fear of judgment. By embracing and celebrating your own quirks, you're helping to create just that.

Of course, deciding to stand out can come with a side of anxiety about how others will react. Will they judge? Will they laugh? Here's where you need to fortify your self-confidence. Start by focusing on what you genuinely like about yourself. Make a list of your positive attributes, not just how you look but what you contribute to the world. Are you compassionate? Are you a problem solver? Write these down and remind yourself of them daily. When you feel good about who you are, others' opinions start to lose their edge. It's like wearing an invisible suit of armor; whatever gets thrown your way just bounces off.

Building this kind of confidence doesn't happen overnight. It's a process, sometimes a challenging one. But every step you take towards accepting yourself is a step away from the fear of judgment. Surround yourself with supportive friends who appreciate you for who you are, not who they think you should be. Their support can be a powerful buffer against negative judgments. And remember, most people are too wrapped up in their own insecurities to truly judge yours as harshly as you might imagine.

Now, let's talk about the perks of letting your true colors shine, especially when it comes to social situations. When you are authentically yourself, you attract people who genuinely get you. These relationships tend to be deeper and more fulfilling because they're based on real recognition and appreciation of each other's true selves. Plus, being genuine opens doors to opportunities that align with your natural passions and interests. Whether it's joining a club that matches your hobbies or taking on roles that suit your skills, being yourself helps you find the specific area where you can thrive.

Expressing yourself isn't just about how you interact; it's also about finding outlets that let your soul sing. Whether it's fashion, art, writing, or music, these are tools not just for self-expression but for communication. They allow you to say, "This is who I am," without even speaking. If you're into fashion, wear that vintage hat or those funky shoes with pride. If art is your thing, fill your spaces with creations that tell your story. Write blog posts, poems, or stories that let others peek into your world. Every stroke, stitch, or stanza is a declaration of your individuality.

Take, for instance, the simple act of customizing your back-pack or your room. These personal touches are expressions of your identity. They tell a story about what matters to you, what you believe in, and what you love. And every time someone appreciates these expressions, it's a reminder that your unique perspective adds value to the world just as much as the more conventional ones.

So, as you navigate the sometimes turbulent waters of teen life, remember that your individuality is not just a trait to be tolerated but celebrated. It's what makes the tapestry of human experience so wonderfully complex and colorful. Embrace it, express it, and watch as it transforms not only your own view of the world but how the world views you.

Quiz: The Art of Being Different - Thriving as Yourself

1. What's the first step to celebrating your uniqueness?

    a. Hiding all your quirks in a secret vault
    b. Recognizing and appreciating what sets you apart
    c. Trying to be a clone of your favorite celebrity

2. How can you overcome the fear of judgment?
    a. Wear an actual suit of armor to school
    b. Focus on what you genuinely like about yourself and remind yourself of these qualities daily
    c. Only talk to your pet rock

3. What's a fun way to express your individuality?
    a. Dressing like everyone else
    b. Customizing your backpack or room with personal touches
    c. Pretending to be a secret agent in disguise

4. Why is it beneficial to be yourself in social settings?
    a. It helps you blend into the background like a chameleon
    b. It attracts people who genuinely get you and creates deeper connections
    c. It makes you invisible

5. What should you do if you have a quirky sense of humor?
    a. Hide it and only laugh in your head
    b. Embrace it and make others laugh with you
    c. Try to be as dull as possible

Answer Key:

1. b) Recognizing and appreciating what sets you apart
2. b) Focus on what you genuinely like about yourself and remind yourself of these qualities daily
3. b) Customizing your backpack or room with personal touches
4. b) It attracts people who genuinely get you and creates deeper connections

5. b) Embrace it and make others laugh with you

~

DAY 20 HANDLING PEER PRESSURE: STAYING TRUE UNDER PRESSURE

Peer pressure—it's like that sneaky character in video games who pops up and tries to sway you off your mission path with tempting shortcuts or risky moves. You know the deal: everyone's doing it, so why shouldn't you? But here's the scoop: not all invitations to join the crowd are as harmless as they seem, and it's crucial to recognize when you're being nudged, pushed, or downright shoved away from your values or comfort zone. Peer pressure isn't always about the big stuff like drugs or skipping school. It can sneak into the everyday corners of your life, like being persuaded to mock someone to fit in or caving to wear something that's not 'you' just to get approval.

Recognizing these moments is the first step in mastering the art of staying true under pressure. Peer pressure can be as loud as a shout or as quiet as a whisper, suggesting you need to act a certain way to be liked or accepted. It can come from friends, classmates, or even people you look up to. But no matter the source, it's your job to stand guard. Start by asking yourself: "Does this feel right? Am I being nudged to betray my own compass?" Awareness is your shield; it gives you the clarity to see the situation for what it is—a test of your authenticity.

Now, let's talk about defense strategies. Imagine you're prepped for a showdown in your favorite game. You wouldn't go in without a plan, right? The same goes here. One solid tactic is having a set of rehearsed responses ready.

These are your verbal armor pieces against peer pressure. If someone's pushing you to try something you're uncomfortable with, a simple, confident "No, thanks, I'm good" can be surprisingly effective. It shows you're firm in your decision without being confrontational. But what if the pressure doesn't back down? That's when you pull out the strategic retreat—remove yourself from the situation. It's not about running away from the battle; it's about choosing not to play a game where the rules are set against you.

Building self-assurance is like leveling up your character. The more confident you are in who you are and what you stand for, the less impact peer pressure will have on you. Start by declaring your strengths and values daily. It could be through affirmations, journaling, or simply setting small, daily challenges that you can achieve. Each success, no matter how small, builds your confidence. It's about reinforcing the idea that you are capable, you have worth, and you don't need to follow the crowd to validate that.

Let's get interactive and really put your skills to the test with some role-playing exercises. Picture this: you're at a party, and someone offers you a drink you know you shouldn't take. How do you respond? Practice this scenario with a friend or even in front of a mirror. Role-play different outcomes—maybe in one, you change the subject smoothly; in another, you explain why you choose to say no. This practice isn't just about preparing for peer pressure; it's about strengthening your ability to stand up for yourself. It's training in the art of staying true to your principles, even when the world seems to be pushing against them.

Handling peer pressure is an ongoing challenge, one that requires you to be alert, prepared, and confident. It's about knowing when to say yes, how to say no, and having the courage to walk your own path, even when others veer off. This isn't just about resisting negative influences; it's about actively choosing to live a life that's true to yourself, one decision at a time. So next time you feel the weight of peer expectations pushing down on you, remember: you have the tools, you know the tactics, and you absolutely have the strength to push back. Keep standing strong, keep your values in clear sight, and keep being unapologetically you.

Journal Prompt: Handling Peer Pressure - Staying True Under Pressure

> Reflect on a time when you faced peer pressure. How did it make you feel, and what did you do in response? Write about whether you stayed true to your values or felt swayed by the pressure. What strategies could you use next time to handle similar situations better? How can you build your confidence to resist peer pressure in the future?

_____

_____

_____

_____

_____

ROLE MODELS AND MENTORS: LEARNING FROM OTHERS' PATHS

Consider assembling a dream team for an epic video game battle; you'd pick characters with top-notch skills, right? Similarly, in life, selecting role models and mentors is about choosing individuals whose achievements and qualities inspire you to grow. It's not just their success that matters, but the values they uphold and the traits they exhibit.

Think about who inspires you—perhaps a tech innovator, a sports icon, or a teacher with engaging classes. What specifically about them motivates you? Is it their creativity, strength, or kindness? Diving into the stories of those you admire offers a behind-the-scenes look at their paths, including both triumphs and setbacks. These narratives show that success is not a straight line but a journey with highs and lows, teaching resilience and adaptability.

For example, understanding how your favorite artist overcame early rejections can highlight the importance of persistence alongside talent. Engaging with mentors can elevate this learning. If you have the opportunity to connect with a mentor, cherish these interactions. Approach them with thoughtful questions that probe deeper than surface-level advice, such as inquiring about the obstacles they've faced and their strategies for overcoming them. This approach not only shows your respect for their insights but also provides you with tailored advice for your own path. Remember, feedback from a mentor is a treasure trove for personal growth, even if it's sometimes challenging to hear.

Consider also how you can embody the role of a mentor or role model for others. You don't need to wait until you're widely recognized; start now by demonstrating kindness, pursuing your passions, and standing up for your beliefs. Your actions can inspire those around you, contributing to a cycle of positive influence and inspiration.

Navigating life with role models and mentors offers guidance through your personal challenges and aspirations, linking you to the broader human experience of striving and achieving. By emulating the paths of those you admire and aspiring to inspire others, you contribute to a legacy of growth and inspiration that exceeds individual achievement. Remember, the figures you look up to were once in your shoes—they dared to dream, persist, and guide others. Now, it's your turn to follow in their footsteps and carve your own path.

As we conclude our journey through individuality and authenticity, remember that embracing your true self and values shapes a life uniquely yours. Discovering passions, living by your values, expressing uniqueness, navigating peer pressure, and learning from role models and mentors are all crucial steps. Each action paints your life's masterpiece.

Continue making bold choices and using vibrant colors. As we move to the next section, take these lessons and inspirations with you, lighting the way to personal growth and fulfillment.

Every leaf on the tree carries a unique pattern, a testament to the beauty of individuality. Embracing one's true self allows the tree to stand tall, its authenticity shining through each distinct branch and leaf.

SECTION 6: FORMING AND MAINTAINING FRIENDSHIPS

"Friendship is born at that moment when one person says to another, 'What! You too? I thought I was the only one."

C.S. LEWIS

Imagine you're crafting the ultimate squad in your favorite multiplayer game. Who do you pick? The unstoppable warrior? The cunning strategist? Or maybe the loyal sidekick? Believe it or not, forming friendships in real life isn't much different. It's about picking the right mix of characters who'll stand by you during boss fights and cheer you on during victory dances. But instead of looking for someone who can wield a virtual sword, you're looking for those who wield kindness, support and a whole lot of laughs. So, how do you assemble your real-life dream team? Let's dive into the nitty-gritty of choosing friends who add value, not drama, to your life.

DAY 21 CHOOSING FRIENDS: QUALITIES OF GOOD FRIENDSHIPS

First things first: your core values. These are the deep-rooted beliefs that shape who you are and what matters most to you —like the code of honor for knights of old or the unwritten rules of conduct for modern-day superheroes. Maybe honesty tops your list, or perhaps it's loyalty or a sense of humor. Understanding your own core values is like having an internal guide; it helps you steer toward people who share similar principles. When you and your friends value the same fundamental ideas, your friendships have a stronger foundation built on mutual respect and understanding. It's like syncing your gameplay so everyone's working toward the same quest—winning together, supporting each other, and having a blast along the way.

Now, let's talk about traits—specifically, the traits that make for a good friend. Reliability is a big one. You want friends who are like that trusty old bike you can always count on to get you where you need to go—no unexpected breakdowns or last-minute bailouts. Kindness is another critical trait. A friend who spreads kindness is like a walking, talking, feel-good playlist, brightening up your days and supporting you when you're down. And let's not forget a supportive nature. A friend who's supportive is like your personal cheerleader, hyping you up for your achievements and cushioning your falls. These traits manifest in everyday interactions, often in small acts like showing up on time, listening with genuine interest, or sending you a meme just when you need a laugh. It's these little things that, when stacked together, form the bedrock of a solid friendship.

But it's not all high-fives and group selfies. There are red flags to watch out for—signals that a potential friend might not be the best addition to your squad. Inconsistency is one such red flag. If someone is your BFF one day and giving you the cold shoulder the next, alarm bells should ring. Disrespect is another major deal-breaker. It's a clear sign that they're not friend material if they don't respect your boundaries, feelings, or others. And beware of anyone who pressures you to conform—true friends celebrate your individuality, not stifle it. Recognizing these red flags early can save you from drama and heartache down the line. It's like spotting a glitch in your favorite game before it crashes your system—you're better off steering clear!

Finally, let's chat about the power of diversity in friendships. Just like a well-rounded team in sports or gaming, having friends from different backgrounds and perspectives can enrich your life immensely. It opens you up to new ideas, experiences, and ways of seeing the world. It's about adding various spices to your friendship stew, making it richer and more flavorful. Embracing diversity in your friendships encourages openness and inclusivity, making your social circle a vibrant tapestry woven from many different threads. Imagine the stories, the insights, the varied laughter—each friend adding their unique color to the palette of your life.

Choosing the right friends is about more than just sharing interests or hanging out. It's about finding people who uplift you, challenge you, and support you as you grow. It's about surrounding yourself with positivity, respect, and joy. So take your time to choose wisely, and remember, the best friendships aren't just about being there for the good times; they're about thriving together, learning from each other, and building connections that last a lifetime. Now, armed with the know-how on what makes a great friend and how to spot the not-so-great ones, you're set to build your own epic squad. Let the adventures begin!

Quiz Choosing Friends - Qualities of Good Friendships

1. What's one of the first steps in choosing good friends?
   a. Picking the person with the coolest collection of rubber ducks
   b. Identifying your core values, like a knight with a code of honor
   c. Seeing who can burp the alphabet the fastest
2. Which trait is essential in a good friend?
   a. Reliability, like a trusty old bike that never gets a flat tire
   b. Inconsistency, like a magician's disappearing rabbit
   c. Disrespect, like a cat knocking things off the table for fun
3. What's a red flag to watch out for in a potential friend?
   a. Consistency in baking delicious cookies
   b. Disrespecting your boundaries, like a nosy alien
   c. Supporting your individuality, like a cheerleading unicorn
4. Why is diversity in friendships important?
   a. It makes your group photo look like a rainbow exploded
   b. It enriches your life with new ideas and experiences, like adding spices to a friendship stew
   c. It ensures everyone agrees that pineapple belongs on pizza
5. How can you tell if someone is a supportive friend?

    a. They only talk about their pet hamster's adventures

    b. They celebrate your achievements with confetti and pom-poms

    c. They ignore your feelings like a robot programmed for world domination

Answer Key:

1. b) Identifying your core values, like a knight with a code of honor
2. a) Reliability, like a trusty old bike that never gets a flat tire
3. b) Disrespecting your boundaries, like a nosy alien
4. b) It enriches your life with new ideas and experiences, like adding spices to a friendship stew
5. b) They celebrate your achievements with confetti and pom-poms

~

DAY 22 BEING A GOOD FRIEND: RESPONSIBILITIES AND REWARDS

Friendships aren't just about having someone to share your fries with or binge-watch the latest series; they're about giving and taking, being there during the rough patches, and celebrating the wins like they're your own. Understanding the dynamics of friendship can sometimes feel like creating a piece of art, where every brushstroke influences the final masterpiece. Let's explore some of the crucial elements that make friendships not just survive but thrive.

Think of friendship as a two-way street where both sides contribute and receive—sort of like a game of catch. You throw the ball, and they catch and throw it back. If you're constantly throwing the ball and it never comes back, that's going to be one boring game, right? That's why giving and taking in friendships is vital. It's about balancing what you offer and what you get. Maybe you're great at listening, and your friend is hilarious and always lifts your spirits. What matters here isn't to keep a ledger but to feel that there's a balance over time, that your efforts and theirs harmonize to create a friendship that's rewarding for both of you. It's about contributing to the friendship willingly without tallying up who did what last. This spontaneous, generous sharing of time, energy, and pizza slices is what solidifies your bond.

Now, let's talk about being there during the tough times. Supporting a friend in need doesn't mean you have to have all the answers or fix their problems. Sometimes, it's about being present, offering a listening ear, or just sitting with them in silence. Listening is a superpower in friendships. It involves really hearing what they're saying without planning your subsequent response or comparing their problems to yours. It's about acknowledging their feelings without rushing to judge or offer unsolicited advice. If they need more than a listening ear, ask how you can help. Maybe they need help studying, a companion for a problematic errand, or just someone to binge-watch their comfort show with. Remember, the aim is not to be their hero but their friend— one who's present but not overbearing.

Celebrating your friends' successes is like cheering for your favorite team—not because you expect something in return, but because their happiness genuinely makes you happy. It could be as big as them winning a national championship or as simple as nailing a tough math test. The act of celebrating each other's achievements creates shared moments of joy, strengthening your connection and deepening your bond. It tells your friend, "I'm with you, and I'm for you," and let's face it, who doesn't want a cheerleader in their corner? These celebrations can be small gestures, like a congratulatory note, a special treat, or just a heartfelt "I'm so proud of you!" It's about recognizing their efforts and showing that what matters to them matters to you, too.

Lastly, a word on boundaries—they're the invisible lines that help each person in a friendship feel safe and respected. Boundaries can range from how often you hang out to the kind of jokes you're okay with to how much you're willing to share about personal topics. Setting and respecting these boundaries are crucial for any healthy relationship. It involves communicating your needs clearly—like saying, "I need some time alone this weekend," or "I'm not comfortable discussing that topic." It's non-negotiable that this communication is a two-way street; you should respect their boundaries just as much as you want yours to be respected. Healthy boundaries help prevent feeling overwhelmed or taken advantage of, ensuring that the friendship remains a space where both of you feel valued and respected.

Journal Prompt: Being a Good Friend: Responsibilities and Rewards

> Reflect on a friendship in which you feel a good balance of give and take. Describe a recent situation in which you supported your friend, or they supported you. How did this experience strengthen your bond?
>
> Next, think about a time when you celebrated a friend's success. How did you celebrate, and how did it make both of you feel? What are

some ways you can continue to show
support and celebrate your friends'
achievements?

Lastly, consider the boundaries in your friendships. Are there areas where you feel
comfortable setting more clear boundaries?
How can you communicate these boundaries to ensure mutual respect and understanding?

Write about the responsibilities and rewards of
being a good friend and how these elements
contribute to thriving, fulfilling friendships.

_____

_____

_____

_____

_____

DAY 23 GROUP DYNAMICS: FINDING YOUR PLACE

Are you the one who is always planning the hangouts (hello,
leader!), or perhaps you're the peacemaker when drama
strikes (yep, you're the mediator)? Understanding group
dynamics is like figuring out where you fit on a sports team

or in a band. Everyone has a role that helps the group vibe well and achieve its goals, whether that's having a blast at prom or acing a group project.

First up, let's break down some typical roles you might find in any group. There's the leader, often the one who sets directions and gets everyone pumped. Think of them as the quarterback in football, always keeping an eye on the end zone. Then there's the mediator, the one who smooths over conflicts and keeps the peace. They're like the calm yoga instructor who keeps everyone zen. The motivator is up next, always cheering the group on and making sure everyone feels included and valued, kind of like the hype person in a rap battle. And don't forget the innovator, who's always got a million ideas and sees solutions where others see problems. Identifying your natural role in a group setting isn't just about sticking to one lane; it's about knowing how you can best contribute to the group's success and harmony.

But what if you're not sure about your role? No big deal. Try observing how you behave in different group settings. What actions feel most natural to you? Do you find yourself offering solutions, keeping spirits high, or maybe ensuring everyone sticks to the plan? These clues can hint at your natural role within the group. And remember, roles can evolve. You may start out as a follower, learning the ropes. Still, as you get more comfortable, you may become a leader or an idea generator.

Now, onto a trickier part of group dynamics—peer pressure. It's like that sneaky level in a video game where everything seems fine, and then bam, you're facing a boss fight you didn't see coming. Standing firm on your values is your best defense. It helps to have a clear sense of your morals and what you're comfortable with. This way, you're ready with your shield when someone tries to sway you into skipping class or gossiping. Practice saying no in a firm yet polite way. You could say something like, "I appreciate the invite, but I'm not really into that." Remember, true friends will respect your choices, even if they're different from theirs.

Creating an inclusive group is like hosting a party where everyone feels welcome. It starts with being a good host. Introduce people to each other, highlight common interests, and create opportunities for everyone to shine. Please pay attention to who might feel left out and make an effort to bring them into the fold. For instance, ask for their opinion if you notice someone is quiet during a group discussion. Sometimes, all it takes is a simple, "Hey, Casey, you're quiet today. What do you think?" to make someone feel seen and valued.

If you spot exclusion happening, whether it's subtle or outright, it's crucial to address it. This doesn't mean calling someone out in front of everyone (which can backfire) but instead having a private conversation about how inclusivity makes for a more substantial, happier group. Share how various thoughts and backgrounds can lead to more creative and effective collaboration. After all, a group where everyone feels included is not just a nicer place to be; it's also more successful and engaged.

Balancing individual friendships within a larger group can be like juggling. You want to spend time with everyone, but you also don't want anyone to feel like they're just part of the crowd. It's vital to nurture individual relationships within the group setting. This might mean grabbing coffee with one friend or hitting the gym with another. These one-on-one hangouts can strengthen each friendship and prevent anyone from feeling like they're lost in the group shuffle.

Sometimes, private bonds can create tension in the larger group, especially if others feel excluded or if inside jokes go too far. It's vital to be mindful of how these private bonds affect group dynamics. Strive to make everyone feel included, especially during group gatherings. Share stories or jokes that everyone can enjoy, and avoid cliques that can split the group. Remember, a tight-knit group isn't about everyone being best friends with each other; it's about everyone feeling respected and included in the collective adventure.

Activity: Finding Your Place in Group Dynamics

Superhero Reflection: Think about a recent group activity or project you were part of. Reflect on your behavior. Imagine your role as a superhero persona. Write a short paragraph about your "superpowers" in the group. For example, if you're a Leader, you might be "Captain Direction," always steering the team toward success.

Peer Pressure Comic: Draw a simple comic strip showing a scenario where you face peer pressure (e.g., being pushed to skip class). Include your superhero persona standing firm against the pressure. Use speech bubbles to write your response.

Inclusivity Challenge: Plan an "Inclusivity Scavenger Hunt" for your next group activity. Create a list of actions to include everyone, such as:

- Ask a quiet member their opinion.
- Invite everyone to join a group game.
- Compliment someone on their contribution.

- Check off each action during your group activity and see how many you can complete.

Friendship Mix-and-Match: Identify one friend in your group you haven't spent much one-on-one time with recently. Plan a fun, creative activity with them, like baking cookies, going on a mini adventure, or creating a playlist together. Give your plan a catchy title, like "Operation Bestie Bonding."

PARTIES AND SOCIAL GATHERINGS: MINGLING LIKE A PRO

Stepping into a party can be overwhelming, but you can navigate these social scenes like a pro with a few tricks.

To join a conversation, wait for a natural break, such as after a laugh or a story, and then chime in with a light comment or question. For example, "That sounds hilarious, what happened next?" introduces you without intrusion. Exiting a chat is just as necessary; do so by expressing your move positively, "I'm off to grab some refreshments, enjoyed our chat!"

Parties require mobility. Move around to increase your visibility and accessibility, making it easier for others to approach you. Introducing yourself is critical. A simple "Hi, I'm [Your Name]," accompanied by a smile, opens the door for interaction. Engage further by asking open-ended questions or offering compliments to find common ground quickly.

Combat social anxiety by preparing mentally. Use breathing exercises to calm your nerves before social encounters and set small, achievable goals for yourself, like talking to three new people. This approach helps focus your energy away from anxiety and towards positive interactions.

Understanding both others' and your own body language enhances communication. If someone seems disengaged, give them space. Conversely, open body language from you or others usually indicates interest and receptiveness to the conversation. By mastering the art of conversation, moving with purpose, managing anxiety, and reading social cues, you'll find yourself enjoying social gatherings more, making new friends, and creating lasting memories.

$\sim$

DAY 24 COMMUNICATING IN CONFLICTS: KEEPING FRIENDSHIPS STRONG

Have you ever found yourself in the middle of a heated game where suddenly, what was a friendly match turns into a virtual battlefield? It's incredible how quickly things can spiral out of control, right? Well, conflicts in friendships can feel pretty similar. One minute, you're joking around, and the next, you're both hurling words like digital missiles. But here's the kicker: resolving conflicts doesn't have to be about winning or losing. It's about understanding, adjusting, and moving forward stronger. Let's gear up and dive into some strategies to help you keep your friendships as strong as a fortified castle, even when disagreements try to breach the walls.

First up: healthy conflict resolution. Picture this: you and your friend are at odds over which movie to watch. You're dying to watch the latest superhero flick while they're in the mood for a horror marathon. Instead of the classic "But I picked last time!" or the silent treatment, try using "I" statements. It's a game-changer. Start with, "I feel like we always end up watching what you want, and I'd really appreciate it if we could find a compromise." This way, you're expressing your feelings without blaming them and opening up the floor for a healthy discussion. It's like sending a peace envoy to negotiate terms – it keeps the doors of communication open. It reduces the chance of things getting messy.

Active listening is another vital player in this scenario. This means really listening to what they're saying, not just planning your next argument while they speak. Maybe they had a terrible day and are looking for some predictable scares to unwind. Finding a middle ground becomes easier when you understand where they're coming from. Maybe agree to watch a bit of both genres? By actively listening and responding with kindness, you turn a potential confrontation into a win-win situation, keeping the friendship on solid ground.

Now, let's tackle de-escalating arguments before they turn into full-blown wars. It's all about catching the tension early and hitting the brakes. Imagine you're in a heated discussion that's rapidly going south. Suggest taking a timeout instead of throwing fuel on the fire with sarcastic remarks or hurtful comments. Literally say, "Let's take a few minutes to cool down." It's like hitting the pause button on a tense gameplay, giving both of you time to breathe and collect your thoughts. When emotions are running high, stepping back can prevent saying things you might regret and helps maintain the respect that's so crucial in any relationship.

After cooling down, approaching the discussion with a clear, calm mind can make a huge difference. Think of it as re-entering the game with a new strategy after realizing the old one wasn't working. Discuss calmly and clearly what bothered you, listen to the other person's side, and try to find a solution that respects both perspectives. Sometimes, just the act of calmly discussing an issue can make all the difference, turning a potential friendship-ending argument into a moment of mutual understanding and respect.

Moving on is part of any strong friendship: the ability to apologize and forgive. Let's say you dropped the ball — maybe you forgot their birthday or accidentally spilled a secret. Owning up to your mistakes and offering a sincere apology can go a long way. A simple, heartfelt "I'm really sorry I hurt you; that wasn't my intention" shows maturity and respect for the friendship. It's about acknowledging your blunder and showing that you care enough to make amends.

On the flip side, forgiving a friend who genuinely apologizes is equally important. Holding onto grudges is like lugging a heavy backpack during a hike; it just makes the journey more challenging. Forgiving doesn't mean forgetting; it means choosing to move forward. It helps rebuild trust and respect, which are the foundation of any strong relationship. Remember, everyone makes mistakes, and forgiveness is a gift that heals both the giver and the receiver.

Finally, let's talk about turning lemons into lemonade. Conflicts, when handled properly, can actually strengthen friendships. They're like the challenging moments in a group project that push you to work together and improve. Each disagreement gives you insights into each other's boundaries, expectations, and communication styles. For instance, you might learn that your friend hates being teased in public or that they need some time to think before discussing an issue. These insights are valuable; they help you understand each other better, paving the way for a more considerate and connected relationship.

So, next time you find yourself in a disagreement, look at it as an opportunity to improve your friendship. Discuss openly what you both can learn from the experience and how you can prevent similar conflicts in the future. Maybe you establish a code word that means, "This is important to me; let's discuss this calmly," or you always agree to take a break and revisit the conversation with a clear mind. These strategies not only solve the immediate problem but also bolster your friendship against future storms, making sure that your ship sails smoothly even when the waters get rough.

Quiz: Communicating in Conflicts - Keeping Friendships Strong

1. What's a healthy way to start a discussion when you and a friend disagree on what movie to watch?
   a. "Rock, paper, scissors for the win!"
   b. "I feel like we always end up watching what you want. Can we compromise?"
   c. "I'm building a fort, and it's superhero-themed. Join or be banished!"
2. What's the best approach when your friend is talking about their bad day and you're in a disagreement?
   a. Interrupt with, "Hey, let's talk about me now!"
   b. Actively listen and respond with kindness.
   c. Pretend you're a detective solving a mystery: "Interesting, tell me more about this 'terrible day.'"
3. How can you de-escalate a heated argument with a friend?
   a. Suggest a timeout and take a few minutes to cool down.

    b. Challenge them to a thumb war to settle it.

    c. Start a dance-off to release the tension.

4. What's an important step when you realize you've made a mistake and hurt your friend?

    a. Apologize sincerely: "I'm really sorry I hurt you. That wasn't my intention."

    b. Blame your imaginary twin for the mistake.

    c. Distract them with a magic trick: "Look over here, nothing up my sleeve!"

5. Why is forgiving a friend who apologizes important?

    a. It restores trust and helps move forward.

    b. It gives you a free pass to tease them about it forever.

    c. It's a perfect opportunity to invent a new secret handshake.

Answer Key:

1. b) "I feel like we always end up watching what you want. Can we compromise?"
2. b) Actively listen and respond with kindness.
3. a) Suggest a timeout and take a few minutes to cool down.
4. a) Apologize sincerely: "I'm really sorry I hurt you. That wasn't my intention."
5. a) It restores trust and helps move forward.

∾

DAY 25 WHEN TO WALK AWAY: RECOGNIZING TOXIC RELATIONSHIPS

Let's face it: Not all friendships are meant to last forever, but that's okay. It's like clearing out your playlist; sometimes, you have to remove a few tracks that no longer make you feel good. Recognizing when a friendship turns toxic—meaning it consistently drains your happiness or undermines your well-being—is crucial for maintaining your mental health. A toxic relationship can be laced with manipulation, constant negativity, or disrespect. These aren't just bad days that everyone has; these are patterns that make you feel worse after every interaction. A friend who manipulates you might twist your words, make you feel guilty for things that aren't your fault, or even try to control your decisions. Persistent negativity from a friend can look like constant criticism, cynicism about your dreams, or pitting you against your own values. Disrespect might come through in dismissive behaviors, ignoring your boundaries, or ridiculing your interests. Recognizing these traits is the first step in protecting your well-being.

Now, how do you know when it's time to walk away? Imagine your energy as a battery—some interactions might recharge you, while others could drain you dry. If you consistently feel depleted after hanging out with someone or if you notice your self-esteem dropping faster than your phone's battery life, those are big red flags. Another sign is if you find your boundaries being repeatedly trampled. For instance, if you've expressed discomfort about certain jokes and they keep making them anyway, that's a clear sign of disrespect. Trust your gut here. If something feels off, it probably is. Lack of trust is another deal-breaker. If you're second-guessing their intentions more often than not, or if you think you can't rely on them in the moments it matters, the foundation of your friendship might be shaky.

Ending a friendship, especially a long-standing one, can feel as daunting as quitting a long-term job. You might worry about the aftermath or whether you're making the right decision. However, just like in any breakup, clarity and respect are a must-have. Plan what you want to say beforehand. You might start with something like, "I've been feeling [insert feelings] about our friendship for a while, and I think it's best for me to step back." Be honest, but also be compassionate. You're not trying to win an argument but to close a section peacefully. Stick to "I" statements to express your feelings without unnecessarily blaming the other person. This isn't about their character flaws; it's about how the relationship isn't working for you.

After you've parted ways, it's necessary to dive into some serious self-care. Think of it as emotional first aid. This could be anything from spending time with people who recharge your batteries to picking up hobbies that you might have put aside. Allow yourself to grieve the loss of the friendship. It's okay to feel sad, confused, or even relieved. Processing these emotions is part of healing. Don't rush into new friendships right away. Give yourself the space to understand what went wrong and what you truly value in friendships. This reflection will help you build healthier friendships in the future, ones that uplift and support you just as much as you do them.

Navigating friendships isn't always straightforward. It involves a lot of trial and error, adjustments, and sometimes, tough decisions like ending a friendship. However, each interaction, each connection, and each conclusion teaches you more about who you are and what you value in relationships. As you move forward, you'll find that the friendships that do stick around are those that bring out the best in you and you in them.

Journal Prompt: When to Walk Away: Recognizing Toxic Relationships

Reflect on a friendship that has made you feel consistently unhappy or drained. Write about specific behaviors or patterns that have made you feel this way. How have these interactions impacted your well-being and self-esteem?

Next, consider the signs that suggest it might be time to walk away from this friendship. Do you feel your boundaries are being ignored or your trust is consistently broken?

Finally, think about how you would approach ending this friendship. What would you say to express your feelings honestly and respectfully?

Write down some self-care strategies you can use to help you heal and process the end of this friendship. How will you ensure your future friendships are healthy and supportive?

_____

_____

_____

_____

_____

MANAGING CONFLICT: REAL-LIFE STRATEGIES FOR TOUGH SITUATIONS

Conflict is an inevitable part of life, much like an uninvited party guest. It can arise from minor disagreements to major arguments, but you can navigate these challenges effectively with the right strategies.

Assertive communication is needed in resolving conflicts. It involves expressing your thoughts, feelings and needs transparently, openly, and respectfully. Instead of accusing others with "You" statements, use "I" statements to focus on how you feel and what you need. For example, swap "You never listen to me" with "I feel unheard when I'm interrupted." This approach fosters understanding and empathy, paving the way for real solutions.

Aim for win-win solutions where all parties feel they've gained something. Understand the other person's perspective to identify mutual needs and concerns. Be creative in brainstorming solutions that accommodate everyone involved. Whether it's negotiating car usage with a sibling or dividing tasks in a group project, finding common ground is imperative.

Staying calm under pressure is essential. If emotions run high, take a timeout. A brief pause can help you cool down, think clearly, and return to the discussion with a more focused perspective. Managing your emotions prevents minor disagreements from escalating.

After resolving a conflict, reflect on the experience. Consider what triggered the disagreement, how you managed it, and what you learned. This reflection isn't about dwelling on mistakes but about preparing for future conflicts. Every situation offers insights to improve your conflict-resolution skills. In learning to handle conflicts constructively, you not only maintain but also strengthen relationships. Communicating assertively, seeking mutually beneficial solutions, managing emotions, and reflecting on your experiences are all significant steps. Embrace these opportunities for growth and understanding, and approach each conflict as a chance to develop your skills.

Up next, we'll explore how to develop romantic relationships, another complex but rewarding part of your social journey.

As branches intertwine, they symbolize the bonds of friendship —strong, supportive, and ever-growing. The tree shows how these connections, rooted in trust and shared experiences, help it weather any storm.

SECTION 7 DEVELOPING ROMANTIC RELATIONSHIPS

"We accept the love we think we deserve."

STEPHEN CHBOSKY, THE PERKS OF
BEING A WALLFLOWER

I magine you're standing in front of a giant, colorful vending machine, but it's filled with feelings instead of snacks. You put in a coin, press a button, and out pops an emotion. Surprise! You've just selected "Attraction." But wait, what exactly did you get? Is it the fizzy, exciting kind that makes your stomach do somersaults, or is it the deep, soulful variety that feels like a warm blanket on a cold day? Understanding attraction, especially as a teen, can feel a bit like trying to understand a new app—there's a lot going on, and not all of it makes sense at first glance. So let's decode this app of attraction together, shall we?

~

UNDERSTANDING ATTRACTION: MORE THAN JUST FEELINGS

Diving into the science behind attraction, it's fascinating to learn that our brains release a mix of chemicals like dopamine, oxytocin, and adrenaline when we're drawn to someone. These not only make us feel euphoric and attached but also cause physical reactions such as a racing heart. Beyond biology, emotional attraction plays a significant role, influenced by our experiences, personality, and even our mood during the initial meeting. This explains why we might feel a strong pull towards someone who doesn't fit our typical "type."

Attraction has different layers, including the physical, emotional, and intellectual. While physical attraction focuses on appearance, emotional attraction is about being drawn to someone's personality, and intellectual attraction sparks from shared interests or exciting conversations. These attractions can grow and change, transforming initial physical interest into deeper emotional connections as we get to know someone better.

Distinguishing between attraction and love is paramount; attraction is the initial interest that draws us to someone, while love is a deeper, more committed connection that values the person's well-being and accepts their flaws. Recognizing this difference can guide our decisions in pursuing relationships or appreciating a crush for the excitement it brings.

To manage attraction effectively, it's important to keep perspective and not let it consume your life. Slow down to truly understand your feelings and the nature of your attraction, communicate openly, and reflect on what you appreciate about the person beyond just their appearance.

Managing attraction thoughtfully is fundamental in developing healthy, fulfilling relationships and understanding ourselves and our partnership values.

~

DAY 26 HEALTHY DATING PRACTICES: RESPECT AND CONSENT

So, you're considering stepping into the dating scene, or maybe you're already knee-deep in it. Either way, navigating the waters of romantic relationships is a bit like learning to drive. There are rules to follow, signals to understand, and it's necessary to respect the other 'drivers' on the road. Let's break down the essentials of healthy dating practices, which are all about respect, honesty, and, of course, a good dose of mutual understanding.

Diving headfirst into dating without understanding the basics of respectful relationships is like trying to run before you can walk—it's likely to lead to some trips and falls. The cornerstone of any healthy relationship is respect. This means valuing each other's opinions, feelings, and boundaries. It's about listening to your partner and treating their views with the same level of importance as your own. Honesty plays a huge role, too. Being upfront about your feelings and intentions sets the stage for a clear and trusting relationship. This isn't just about avoiding lies; it's about being open about what you're looking for in a relationship, whether it's something casual or more serious.

Consideration is another big one. Understanding and caring for each other's emotional and physical well-being can make all the difference. This means being mindful of what makes your partner comfortable and what doesn't and never intentionally pushing those boundaries. It's about making sure that the relationship is a space where both of you feel safe, valued, and heard. Think of it as a two-player game where both players need to be enjoying themselves for the game to continue successfully.

Now, let's talk about the most indispensable must-have in any relationship: consent. Consent in dating, just like in any other situation, is all about agreement and voluntary participation. It's crucial in all aspects of dating, from holding hands to kissing to everything else that couples do. Consent should always be explicit, enthusiastic, and ongoing. This means you need to check in with your partner before moving to a new level in your relationship. A simple "Is this okay?" can go a long way. And remember, consent, once given, can be withdrawn at any time; it's not a one-time checkbox.

Teaching teens like yourself how to give, recognize, and respect consent is vital. It helps build relationships on foundations of mutual respect and care. Plus, understanding consent fully prepares you for interactions not just with romantic partners but in all areas of life. It's about confirming that all parties are always comfortable with what's happening and that no one feels pressured or forced.

Clear communication is the backbone of any strong relationship, and part of that communication involves setting expectations. This isn't about laying down rules for each other but rather about sharing what you both hope to get out of the relationship. It's like setting the terms before starting a group project—you want to make sure everyone's on the same page and agrees with the plan. Talk about how often you expect to see each other, what your ideas of a perfect date might be, and how you view your relationship growing. These conversations can help prevent misunderstandings and ensure that both partners feel comfortable and respected.

Lastly, peer pressure. It's like the annoying pop-up ads of your social life; it's there, and you have to deal with it, but you don't have to click on it. As a teen, you might feel pressure to start dating, engage in physical intimacy, or stay in a relationship that feels wrong just because it seems like everyone else is doing it. The key here is to stick to your personal values and comfort levels. Remember, dating is personal and subjective. What works for someone else might not work for you, and that's perfectly okay. If you feel pressured, talk about it with someone you trust—a friend, a family member, or a counselor. They can offer you perspective and support, helping you to stand firm in your decisions.

Navigating dating as a teen is no small feat—it's filled with excitement, new experiences, and, of course, its fair share of challenges. By building your relationships on the foundations of respect, honesty, and consent, setting clear expectations, and managing peer pressure, you're setting yourself up for healthier and happier romantic experiences. Remember, every relationship, just like every person, is unique. Take things at your own pace, respect yourself and your partner, and don't be afraid to speak up for what you believe in or need.

Quiz: Understanding Consent in Romantic Relationships

1. What does consent mean in a romantic relationship?
   a. Guessing your partner's feelings
   b. Clearly and willingly agreeing to a specific activity
   c. Doing whatever you think they want
2. When should you ask for consent?

    a. Only the first time you do something new

    b. Every time, before engaging in any activity

    c. Once you've been dating for a month

3. What should you do if your partner says "no" to an activity?

    a. Respect their decision and stop immediately

    b. Try to persuade them to change their mind

    c. Ignore it and proceed anyway

4. Can consent be withdrawn after it has been given?

    a. Yes, at any time

    b. No, once given, it can't be taken back

    c. Only in certain situations

5. Which of these is an example of explicit consent?

    a. Silence

    b. A hesitant "maybe"

    c. An enthusiastic "yes"

6. What is not a valid reason to assume consent?

    a. They agreed to something similar before

    b. They haven't said "no"

    c. They are smiling and seem comfortable

7. What should you do if your partner looks uncomfortable but hasn't said anything?

    a. Continue and hope they're okay with it

    b. Stop and ask if they're comfortable

    c. Assume they're fine since they haven't objected

8. Why is it important to talk about boundaries and consent in a relationship?

    a. To ensure both partners feel safe and respected

    b. To avoid misunderstandings

    c. Both a and b

9. Can someone give consent if they are under the influence of alcohol or drugs?

    a. Yes, as long as they say "yes"

b. No, being under the influence affects their ability to consent

c. Only if they're not too drunk

10. What's the best way to ensure ongoing consent in a relationship?

a. Check in regularly with your partner and communicate openly

b. Assume it's always there once established

c. Only ask when you're unsure

Answer Key:

1. b) Clearly and willingly agreeing to a specific activity
2. b) Every time, before engaging in any activity
3. a) Respect their decision and stop immediately
4. a) Yes, at any time
5. c) An enthusiastic "yes"
6. b) They haven't said "no"
7. b) Stop and ask if they're comfortable
8. c) Both a and b
9. b) No, being under the influence affects their ability to consent
10. a) Check in regularly with your partner and communicate openly

∽

DAY 27 SELF-RESPECT IN RELATIONSHIPS: SETTING BOUNDARIES

So, you're in a relationship, or maybe eyeing one, and you're buzzing with all those feel-good vibes. But let's hit pause for a sec and talk about something super crucial—boundaries. Think of boundaries like your personal rule book; these are your dos and don'ts that help you navigate through relationship waters without losing yourself. It's not about building walls but rather drawing your lines clearly in the sand. Whether it's how much time you spend together, how you handle personal space, or what's cool to share online, setting these personal guidelines is a top priority to keeping any relationship healthy and happy.

Okay, first things first: figuring out your own boundaries. This is about knowing what you're comfortable with physically, emotionally, and digitally. Physically, it might be about how affectionate you are or your comfort level with PDA (public displays of affection). Emotionally, it's about knowing how much of your own feelings and thoughts you're ready to share. And digitally? Well, it's the 21st century, so think about things like whether you're okay with being Instagram official or how much you want to text. Everyone's comfort levels are different, so take some time to think about what feels right for you. Maybe jot down a list or chat about it with a friend to get your thoughts organized.

Now, having boundaries is great, but if they're just rolling around in your head, they're not doing much good. You've got to communicate them to your partner. And nope, this isn't a one-and-done kind of deal; it's an ongoing conversation because relationships evolve, and so might your boundaries. Start the chat with something like, "Hey, can we talk about what we're cool within our relationship?" Keep the tone positive and constructive. It's not about listing demands but rather sharing what makes you feel comfortable and respected. Remember, it's a dialogue, not a monologue, so be ready to listen to their boundaries too.

Once the boundaries are out in the open, respecting them is necessary. It's like each of you has given the other a roadmap to your comfort zones, and it's imperative to stick to the path. If your partner respects your boundaries, awesome! It shows they care about your feelings and comfort. But hey, we're all human, and sometimes people might slip up. If something feels off, gently reminding them about your boundaries is okay. Say something like, "I mentioned before that I'm not cool with that. Can we try another way?" It's all about maintaining respect and understanding that helps both of you feel secure and valued.

But what if the boundary crossings aren't just slip-ups but more of a regular thing? That's where things get a bit more serious. It's essential to assert yourself and remind your partner that your boundaries are non-negotiable. Be clear and firm but also calm. If the boundary-pushing continues, it might be time to seek advice from someone you trust, like a friend, family member, or counselor. They can offer you a fresh perspective and support. Sometimes, if boundaries keep getting ignored, it might even mean reviewing the relationship. Remember, a relationship should bring joy and support into your life, not stress and discomfort.

Navigating boundaries isn't always straightforward, and it can feel a bit awkward at first. But think of it as a central part of any healthy relationship. It's about giving yourself and your partner the space to be yourselves while also growing together. So, take the time to define, communicate, and respect each other's boundaries. By doing so, you're not just building a relationship but also mutual respect and understanding that will help your partnership thrive in the long run. And remember, in any relationship, your feelings and comfort matter just as much as the other person's. So, don't be afraid to speak up. Your boundaries deserve to be respected.

Journal Prompt: Self-Respect in Relationships: Setting Boundaries

Reflect on your personal boundaries in relationships. What physical, emotional, and digital boundaries are essential to you?

Write about a time when you successfully communicated your boundaries. How did you approach the conversation, and what was the outcome?

Consider a situation where your boundaries were not respected. How did you handle it, and what did you learn from the experience?

Finally, list ways you can respect your partner's boundaries. How can you ensure mutual respect and understanding in your relationship?

_____

_____

_____

_____

_____

DAY 28 BALANCING ROMANCE AND FRIENDSHIPS: KEEPING LIFE IN HARMONY

When you start dating someone, it can feel like you've just got your hands on the latest, most exciting video game. Suddenly, every free moment is spent trying to level up in this new relationship. But hold up! What about your squad, the friends who've been with you through thick and thin? It's easy to get so caught up in the whirlwind of a new romance that you might unintentionally sideline your pals. Remember, maintaining a balance between your romantic relationships and friendships isn't just nice; it's necessary. It contributes massively to your overall happiness and stability. Think about it: when your romantic world gets a bit too intense or challenging, who's there to offer a different viewpoint or just a fun distraction? Yep, your friends.

Navigating the delicate art of time management between your partner and your buddies is crucial. It's about giving both your romantic relationships and friendships the time and energy they deserve. Start by looking at your weekly routine—how much time are you dedicating to your significant other versus your friends? Is there a balance, or is one side tipping the scales too much? Consider setting specific days or evenings for friend hangouts and date nights. This way, everyone knows they have their special time with you, and you avoid the pitfalls of last-minute cancellations that can leave someone feeling like a backup plan. Also, communicate openly with both your partner and your friends about your scheduling. Honesty here can prevent misunderstandings and assure all parties that they're valued in your life.

Now, let's chat about the green-eyed monster—jealousy. It can sneak into either type of relationship, stirring up drama. Maybe your friends miss the old days when you were more available, or perhaps your partner feels threatened by your close friendships. Here's where your communication skills need to shine. Address jealousy by bringing it out into the open. If a friend expresses jealousy about the time you're spending with your partner, acknowledge their feelings and reassure them of their importance in your life.

On the other hand, if your partner is feeling uneasy about your friendships, reassure them but also assert your right to have these relationships. It's about validating feelings without compromising your boundaries. Strategies like inviting your partner to join in with your friends sometimes help bridge the gap between your romantic and social lives.

Speaking of which, integrating your significant other into your wider social circles can feel like mixing two different friend groups and hoping they hit it off. Start by choosing neutral, low-pressure settings—think group outings like a beach day or a casual dinner. This allows your partner and your friends to meet on common ground without the pressure to bond instantly. Share with both parties what you value about each of them beforehand; this can pave the way for mutual respect and shared interests to appear naturally. Remember, not everyone has to be best buddies, but mutual respect and friendliness can go a long way in maintaining harmony in your interconnected relationships.

Balancing the scales between your romantic and friend relationships isn't about dividing your time evenly—it's about making sure that the time spent with each is meaningful and satisfying. It's ensuring that you nourish all aspects of your social life without letting one overshadow the other. By fostering this balance, you're not just maintaining relationships; you're enriching them, allowing each to blossom and bring out the best in you. So, as you navigate these dynamics, keep the lines of communication open, prioritize fairness in how you allocate your time, and remember, a well-rounded life includes both great friends and great loves.

Quiz: How to Balance Romance and Friendships

1. What's the first step in managing your time between a romantic partner and friends?
   a. Spend all your free time with your partner
   b. Look at your weekly routine and allocate time for both
   c. Ignore your friends until they complain
2. How can you ensure your friends don't feel sidelined when you start dating someone new?
   a. Set specific days or evenings for friend hangouts
   b. Only hang out with friends when your partner is busy
   c. Cancel plans with friends if your partner calls
3. What's a good way to handle jealousy from friends or your partner?
   a. Ignore their feelings and hope it goes away
   b. Address it openly and reassure them of their importance
   c. Avoid the topic and spend more time alone
4. How can you integrate your significant other into your social circles?
   a. Force them to become best friends with your friends
   b. Choose neutral, low-pressure group outings
   c. Keep your partner and friends completely separate
5. Why is balancing your romantic and friend relationships important?

   a. To ensure that your partner and friends feel equally valued

   b. To prevent feeling overwhelmed by any one relationship

   c. Both a and b

Answer Key:

1. b) Look at your weekly routine and allocate time for both
2. a) Set specific days or evenings for friend hangouts
3. b) Address it openly and reassure them of their importance
4. b) Choose neutral, low-pressure group outings
5. c) Both a and b

~

DEALING WITH BREAKUPS: HEALTHY WAYS TO MOVE ON

Breakups feel like stepping on a LEGO—unexpected and painful. Yet, like challenging levels in a video game, they test our skills and contribute to our growth. Here's how to navigate them with resilience and even gain some insights.

Feeling a whirlwind of emotions is normal post-breakup. It's imperative to express these feelings—through journaling, talking with friends, or even screaming into a pillow. Acknowledge your feelings without dwelling on them too long. Recognize, understand, and gently remind yourself that moving forward is part of the process.

Self-care is a must-have. Maintain your routine, including school and hobbies, and keep a regular sleep schedule. Lean on your support system and try new activities that excite you. Remember, seeking professional help is also a form of self-care, offering additional support when needed.

Every breakup teaches us valuable lessons. Reflect on the relationship to understand your needs and areas for personal growth. This reflection isn't about blame but about learning more about yourself and your desires in a relationship.

Moving on means opening yourself to new possibilities and using the lessons learned to brighten your future. The right time to move on varies for each person. Listen to yourself and move at a pace that feels right for you, ensuring you're moving on for the right reasons. Navigating breakups is hard but also a chance for personal growth. By healthily processing emotions, practicing self-care, learning from the experience, and knowing when you're ready to move on, you're laying the foundation for stronger, healthier future relationships. Remember, each step forward is a step towards a happier, more fulfilled you. As we close this section, we're reminded that life's challenges, including breakups, are pivotal in shaping us into the individuals we're meant to become. Next, we'll delve into handling rejection and failure, continuing to build resilience and confidence.

When the tree bears fruit, it reflects the culmination of nurturing relationships. Just as fruit develops from the union of blossoms and branches, romantic relationships grow from shared care, trust, and mutual growth.

SECTION 8 HANDLING REJECTION AND FAILURE

"I've missed more than 9,000 shots in my career. I've lost almost 300 games. Twenty-six times, I've been trusted to take the game-winning shot and missed. I've failed over and over and over again in my life. And that is why I succeed."

MICHAEL JORDAN

Ever felt like you're stuck in a never-ending audition for the role of "punching Bag' in the blockbuster movie of life, where every rejection hits like an unexpected plot twist? Well, you're not alone in this script. Rejection, whether it's from a crush who ghosted you, a college that sent a rejection letter instead of an acceptance, or friends who traded you for the cool table, rejection can feel like the ultimate plot twist. But here's a little spoiler: it's not really about you. Let's peel back the curtain and see rejection for what it really is—a mismatch of circumstances, not a critique of your awesomeness.

◁◁

IT'S NOT PERSONAL: UNDERSTANDING REJECTION AND FAILURE

Rejection is not a reflection of your worth; it is more like a USB plug not fitting the right port. It's about compatibility, not value. Understanding this helps diminish the sting of rejection, transforming a potentially soul-crushing moment into a simple mismatch to shrug off.

Whether it's being ignored by a crush, left out by friends, or facing academic disappointments, these experiences, although challenging, serve as redirections toward paths more aligned with your journey. They're not stop signs but detours to better-suited avenues.

To manage the emotional whirlwind that rejection can bring, it's imperative to shift your perspective. Instead of seeing it as a sign of personal inadequacy, try to view it as a situational mismatch. Mindfulness exercises can also help by teaching you to acknowledge and observe your feelings without letting them overwhelm you.

Your value isn't defined by external validations like making a team or getting into a specific college. Grounding your self-esteem in your strengths, talents, and meaningful relationships helps you stay resilient. Remember, you are much more than your rejections or failures.

View failure as 'Growth Fuel' rather than a setback. Every failure offers insights, offering you a chance to learn, tweak, and improve. Analyze your failures constructively, focusing on what you can learn rather than dwelling on the negative.

Use your failures as lessons to guide your future actions. If public speaking makes you nervous, join a debate club. If procrastination is your downfall, set gradual goals. It's about applying lessons learned to do better next time.

Risk-taking and experimentation foster growth. Embracing challenges and stepping out of your comfort zone can lead to significant learning opportunities. Every attempt, regardless of its outcome, enriches your understanding and skills. Remember, failure is not the enemy but a guide towards growth and resilience. It's the setbacks that pave the way for comebacks. Keep pushing forward, learning, and daring to explore new paths. Your story is defined not by the failures you encounter but by how you respond to them.

~

DAY 29 SEEKING FEEDBACK: GROWTH FROM CRITICISM

Feedback is like the secret sauce that can turn your plain old burger of efforts into a gourmet masterpiece. But let's be real; it can sometimes taste a bit bitter. The trick is to start seeing feedback as your ally, not your enemy—it's the coach, not the critic. Adopting a positive attitude towards feedback can be a game-changer in your personal and professional growth. Think of it as getting the cheat codes to level up faster and smarter. It's not about someone pointing out your faults; it's about getting insights that can propel you forward. So, how do you turn feedback into your growth superpower? Let's break it down.

First up, getting good at asking for feedback is like learning to mine gold—you need to know where to dig and what tools to use. Start by identifying who to ask. Your best bet is people who regularly observe your performance and whose opinions you respect. This could be a teacher, coach, or even a friend who isn't afraid to give you the real talk. Once you've spotted your feedback providers, it's all about how you frame your request. Instead of a vague "Do you think I did okay?" try a more targeted approach, like, "What's one thing I could improve in my presentations?" Specific questions like this make it easier for people to offer helpful, precise advice rather than general 'good job' platitudes.

Now, receiving feedback can sometimes feel like swallowing a spoonful of wasabi—intense and uncomfortable. However, the real skill lies in interpreting this feedback effectively. Not all feedback will be valuable, and it's crucial to distinguish constructive criticism from less helpful comments. Constructive feedback usually focuses on specific behaviors or actions. It includes suggestions for improvement rather than just pointing out what's wrong. For example, a comment like, "You tend to speak really fast during presentations, which can make it hard to follow," is actionable. It highlights a specific area of improvement rather than just saying, "Your presentation wasn't good."

Once you've sifted through the feedback and picked out the golden nuggets of constructive criticism, the next step is to create an action plan. This is where you turn insight into action. Say you've been told you need to boost your engagement in team projects. Set yourself a goal like, "In the next group project, I will contribute at least three new ideas and ask for feedback from my peers at least twice." Make your goals SMART—Specific, Measurable, Achievable, Relevant, and Time-bound. This approach not only structures your efforts but also makes it easier to track your progress.

Lastly, feedback should be a loop, not a one-off. After implementing the changes based on the initial feedback, go back and ask for more. It's like a game where each level you complete gives you the skills to tackle the next one. Keep the feedback loop going, and you'll find that each round of advice and adjustments brings you closer to mastering the skills you're working on. This ongoing process not only improves your abilities but also deepens your understanding of how you can continue to grow and adapt over time.

In the grand scheme of things, seeking and using feedback effectively are required to turn criticism into stepping stones for success. By learning how to ask the right questions, interpreting the feedback accurately, and taking actionable steps based on the advice, you set yourself up for continuous improvement and success. Remember, every piece of feedback is a perspective that can help you refine your skills and strategies, ensuring that you're not just moving forward but also upward. So next time you get a chance, reach out for that feedback and turn it into your ladder to new heights.

Journal Prompt: Seeking Feedback: Growth from Criticism

Reflect on a recent instance where you received feedback. What was the feedback about, and who provided it? How did you feel when you first received it?

Identify the constructive elements in the feedback and how you can turn them into actionable steps for improvement.

Write down a plan to seek feedback regularly.

Who will you ask, and what specific questions will you pose to get valuable insights?
Consider how you can maintain a positive attitude towards feedback and use it for continuous growth. What strategies will you implement to view feedback as a tool for success?

RESILIENCE BUILDING: BOUNCING BACK STRONGER

Resilience is your emotional armor, the force that propels you forward after setbacks like a bad grade, a breakup, or a rough day. It's essential for weathering life's storms, enabling you to face challenges head-on. Unlike a phone at 1% battery seeking a charger, resilience ensures you're always powered up for what life throws your way.

Cultivating resilience means embracing a growth mindset— viewing challenges as opportunities to develop rather than impossible barriers. Mistakes and failures become lessons that enhance your skills, pushing you to see beyond current obstacles.

Take inspiration from resilience icons like Malala Yousafzai and LeBron James. Malala transformed her recovery into a global advocacy for girls' education, while LeBron turned early career criticisms into a motivator for success. Their stories exemplify how resilience can convert hardships into stepping stones for advancement, not just a return to the status quo.

Building resilience is an ongoing process, with journaling as a foundational practice. It's more than airing frustrations; it's about acknowledging achievements and expressing gratitude. Regularly jotting down positive experiences shifts focus from negatives to positives, strengthening your psychological resilience. This habit acts like an emotional savings account, ready for withdrawal in tough times.

Incorporating these strategies reshapes your perspective on life's challenges, viewing them as integral to your personal growth. Whether it's finding your inner Malala or LeBron, adopting a growth mindset, or chronicling your journey through journaling, each step fortifies your resilience. Embrace every obstacle as a chance to demonstrate your strength. Keep pushing forward, grow more robust, and let resilience guide you.

$\sim$

DAY 30 MOVING FORWARD: MAINTAINING MOTIVATION AFTER A FALL

So, you've hit a bump in the road, maybe even tumbled into a metaphorical ditch along your path to greatness. It happens! The real trick isn't just getting out of the ditch; it's how you dust yourself off and keep marching toward your dreams with the same pep in your step. Keeping your eyes on the prize, or in less cliché terms, maintaining a focus on your long-term goals, can turn these temporary setbacks into mere blips on your radar. It's about seeing the bigger picture. Every stumble feels like a wall when you're fixated only on the immediate hurdles. Still, with your gaze fixed on the horizon, every fall is just one step in a much grander journey.

Think of your long-term goals as your personal North Star, guiding you through dark skies and stormy weather. Whether it's acing your exams, becoming captain of the debate team, or simply improving your social circles, these aren't just checkboxes on your to-do list; they are stepping stones to the future you are building. Keep these visions clear in your mind. Visualize achieving these goals; what does it look like? How does it feel? This isn't just daydreaming; it's a technique used by athletes, entrepreneurs, and artists alike to keep their focus laser-sharp. Visualization can be a powerful motivator, especially when the going gets tough. It's like keeping a photo of the finish line in your pocket as you run the race.

Now, let's jazz up your motivational techniques with some actionable strategies. Affirmations might sound a bit out there, but trust me, giving yourself a daily pep talk can boost your spirits and your confidence. Start your day by telling yourself something positive. It could be, "I am capable of handling whatever comes my way," or "I am continuously moving towards my goals." It's about setting a positive tone for the day and strengthening your belief in yourself. Then, break down your primary goals into smaller, bite-sized pieces. These are your short-term goals, and they should be specific and achievable. Instead of "Get better at math," try "Complete two extra math problems every day." These mini-goals are quick wins that keep your motivational fires burning. Each small victory builds your confidence and propels you further towards your larger ambitions.

But let's be honest: motivation isn't a solo journey. It's a team sport, and your support system—friends, family, mentors—plays a role. These are the cheerleaders in your personal arena, the ones who lift you up when you're down and cheer the loudest when you succeed. Lean on them. Share your frustrations and your triumphs. Sometimes, just talking about a setback can lighten your load and open up perspectives you hadn't considered. These people believe in you; their faith can help bolster your own, especially when your spirits are flagging.

Self-compassion is another major factor in maintaining motivation. Be kind to yourself. Understand that failure is a universal experience; it doesn't single you out as unworthy or incapable. Treat yourself with the same kindness you would offer a friend in your shoes. Practice mindfulness to stay present and grounded, appreciating your efforts regardless of the outcome. Remember, being hard on yourself is like trying to grow a garden by pouring salt into the soil—it just doesn't work. Nurture your garden with patience and kindness, and watch as it returns to bloom, more vibrant than before.

So, as you move forward, remember that maintaining motivation isn't about pushing yourself relentlessly toward perfection. It's about moving confidently towards your goals, armed with a clear vision, actionable plans, and an unshakeable support network. It's about being your own biggest supporter, treating setbacks as lessons, and continuously moving forward, one step at a time.

Activity: Personal North Star Visualization

Sit comfortably in a quiet space where you won't be disturbed.

Close your eyes and take a few deep breaths to center yourself.

Imagine your long-term goals as clearly as possible. Picture the steps you must take to achieve them and the result.

Write down how achieving these goals makes you feel. Use descriptive words to capture the emotions and sensations.

Draw a simple image or symbol that represents your North Star (your ultimate goal). Place it somewhere you'll see daily.

As this final section closes, remember the essence of what it means to keep pushing forward. It's about more than just overcoming obstacles; it's about evolving with each experience, armed with a better understanding of yourself and a refined approach to your goals. Keep your eyes on the horizon, your support close, and your internal dialogue positive. Stay tuned, stay motivated, and, most importantly, stay true to your path. The journey continues with a bonus section, which contains three practical applications and everyday scenarios.

In autumn, the tree sheds its leaves, a natural cycle that mirrors handling rejection and failure. The shedding is not an end but a preparation for renewal, as the tree draws strength from within to emerge stronger in the next season.

BONUS: 3 PRACTICAL APPLICATION AND EVERYDAY SCENARIOS

"Don't let the noise of others' opinions drown out your own inner voice."

STEVE JOBS

I magine you're about to deliver a presentation in front of your class. Your palms are sweaty, and the pressure is on. It's not just any moment—it's your time to shine. Excelling in a presentation can feel as rewarding as winning a significant game. However, triumph requires skill-building first. Let's explore how to confidently communicate, engage your classmates, and manage nerves effectively.

～

BONUS 1: ACING SCHOOL PRESENTATIONS WITH CONFIDENCE

Think of preparing for a presentation like planning a road trip—you wouldn't start without a map, snacks, and tunes. Similarly, outline your presentation with a clear start, middle, and end to structure your talk like a story. Practice aloud to get comfortable with your delivery, smoothing out any "umms" or awkward gestures, and ensure your content fits the allotted time.

Start with a strong hook—a surprising fact or bold statement —to capture attention. Maintain eye contact to connect with your classmates, using rhetorical questions and vivid language to keep them engaged. Avoid jargon to ensure clarity and keep your audience hooked.

Feeling nervous is natural and indicates you care. Use deep breathing to calm your mind, and visualize a successful outcome to boost confidence. Embrace the adrenaline to energize your presentation, making it more compelling.

Value feedback from teachers and peers as a tool for growth. Listen actively, seek specifics to understand your strengths and areas for improvement, and apply this insight to refine your skills. Receiving feedback is a chance to see where you shine and where to focus your efforts. Mastering school presentations goes beyond not fumbling through slides—it's about captivating your audience, managing anxiety, and leveraging feedback to enhance your communication skills. With these strategies, you're set to deliver outstanding presentations.

BONUS 2: NAILING YOUR FIRST JOB INTERVIEW

Stepping into your first job interview feels like the spotlight's on you, not for a performance, but for a chance to kickstart your career. Success here goes beyond luck; it's about preparation and making a memorable impression.

Start by thoroughly researching the company. Dive deep into its website to understand its projects and values. This knowledge lets you tailor your responses, showing you're not just a candidate but a potential asset who aligns with its vision. Preparation extends to anticipating interview questions. Instead of memorizing answers, craft thoughtful responses that reflect your skills and experiences, making sure they're relevant to the position. This approach turns the nerve-wracking interview questions into opportunities to showcase your strengths confidently.

First impressions begin the moment you arrive. Dress appropriately and arrive 10-15 minutes early to show your punctuality and eagerness. Greet your interviewer with a firm handshake and a friendly smile to set a positive tone from the start.

Employ the STAR technique for behavioral questions, structuring your answers to highlight your problem-solving and critical-thinking skills. STAR stands for Situation, Task, Action, and Result. Begin by describing the **Situation** you were in, then explain the **Task** you needed to accomplish. Next, outline the specific **Actions** you took to address the task, and finally, share the **Results** of those actions, emphasizing any positive outcomes. This method ensures your responses are clear, concise, and impactful.

Don't forget the follow-up. A thank-you email post-interview not only shows good manners but also reiterates your interest in the position and highlights the main points from your conversation, keeping you fresh in the interviewer's mind. Remember, acing your first job interview is about detailed preparation, making a strong initial impact, effectively structuring your answers, and thoughtful follow-up. These steps are not just about landing the job but laying the groundwork for a successful career with confidence and skill.

$\sim$

BONUS 3: VOLUNTEERING - A PATH TO ENHANCED SOCIAL SKILLS

Volunteering is your secret level in the social skills video game. It's not just about boosting your resume; it's about making impactful contributions, enhancing teamwork, and expanding your network. Think of yourself as a matchmaker, aligning your passions with meaningful causes. Whether it's supporting animal welfare, conserving the environment, or aiding a food bank, find what ignites your passion.

Start with identifying what matters to you and then connect with organizations that share your values. Remember, the ideal match benefits both you and the cause, offering skills, friendships, and new perspectives.

Teamwork is vital in volunteering. It's about uniting diverse skills and personalities towards a common goal. Effective communication, including active listening and respectful dialogue, ensures a harmonious effort. Embrace varied roles, whether leading or following, as each offers valuable lessons. Acknowledging teammates' efforts fosters a supportive environment, motivating everyone to contribute their best.

View every volunteer opportunity as a networking event. You might meet future employers, mentors, or friends, opening doors to further opportunities. Approach each experience with professionalism and enthusiasm, making lasting impressions. Engage with a diverse group of people, learning from every interaction and potentially unlocking recommendations or introductions in your field.

Volunteering is more than accumulating service hours; it's about contributing to societal improvement. Your efforts, no matter how small, are part of a more significant movement for change. The skills and experiences gained through volunteering not only enhance your personal development but also prepare you for future challenges.

As you seek to expand your social skills, consider volunteering. It's an avenue for growth, networking, and making a real-world impact. Dive into causes you're passionate about, collaborate with teams, and connect with the community. Volunteering offers a unique platform for personal and social development.

∼

REFLECTING ON GROWTH: REVIEWING YOUR 30-DAY JOURNEY

So, you've been on this wild ride for 30 days, diving deep into the social jungle, and now it's time to pull over and check your map. How far have you come? What new territories of your personality did you discover? Reflecting on your growth isn't just about giving yourself a pat on the back—it's about understanding what worked, what didn't, and how you can continue evolving. So, let's break down some nifty techniques to help you gauge your progress and plan your next moves. Think of this as your personal "level-up" checkpoint.

Self-Assessment Techniques

Self-assessment is like being your own coach. You get to ask the tough questions, cheer on the wins, and strategize over the losses. Start by revisiting the goals you set at the beginning of this guide. Did you reach them? Did they change as you progressed? This isn't just about ticking boxes; it's about understanding why some goals were met and others weren't.

For each goal, consider what skills or actions helped you succeed or what barriers stood in the way. Maybe you found that speaking up in groups became more natural with practice, or perhaps you realized that time management still trips you up. Whatever the case, each insight is a nugget of gold for your personal development stash.

To structure this reflection, you might use a simple grid method: write down each goal, what you achieved, what you learned, and what you still need to work on. This visual layout can help you see patterns in your growth and areas that need more attention. It's like a snapshot of your current skill landscape, showing you where the fertile fields lie and where the ground is still a bit rocky.

Journaling Reflections

If you've been keeping a journal these past 30 days (and if you haven't, there is no time like the present to start!), now's the time to flip back through those pages. Your journal is more than a collection of daily entries; it's a map of your mental and emotional evolution.

Look for changes in how you describe your interactions and feelings. Are you more confident in certain areas? Do you notice a shift in how you handle stress or setbacks? This isn't about judging your feelings but understanding them. It's decoding the language of your own mind and heart, which can teach you heaps about how you react and adapt to various situations.

Journaling can also highlight the moments that brought you joy, success, or pride. These are the gems that sometimes get buried in the hustle of daily challenges. Maybe you had a breakthrough in a conversation with a friend or managed a project more smoothly than ever before. Celebrate these victories! They are as much a part of your journey as the struggles.

Setting Future Goals

Now, armed with fresh insights and a clearer understanding of your strengths and weaknesses, it's time to set some new goals. But let's mix it up this time. Set some 'stretch goals' alongside your personal development goals—challenges that push you just beyond the edge of your comfort zone. If networking makes you nervous, maybe your next goal is to attend a social event or join a club. If you struggled with speaking up in class, perhaps you aim to ask or answer a question in every class for a week.

Remember, these goals should be SMART: Specific, Measurable, Achievable, Relevant, and Time-bound. This framework isn't just academic fluff; it's a proven strategy that gives your ambitions a precise shape and an actionable path. It's like programming your GPS for a new destination. You know exactly where you want to go and how you plan to get there.

Celebrating Achievements

Every step forward, no matter how small, is a step worth celebrating. Don't wait for the big wins to give yourself a high-five. Celebrated achievements fuel your journey, boosting your motivation and confidence. Maybe treat yourself to a movie night after a week of meeting your new goals, or share your progress with a friend or family member. These celebrations reinforce the positivity of your efforts and remind you that growth is not just possible; it's happening.

As you wrap up this reflection phase, remember that growth is a continuous journey, not a destination. Each day brings new challenges and opportunities to learn and improve. So, take a moment to appreciate how far you've come, and get excited about where you're headed next. The skills you've developed, the insights you've gained, and the goals you've set are all stepping stones to the next section of your personal and social development. Keep pushing forward, aiming high, and turning everyday interactions into opportunities for growth. The journey continues, and the best is yet to come!

CONCLUSION

Well, here we are at the finish line of our 30-day social skill marathon! You've sprinted through the basics of sparkling conversation, hurdled over social anxiety, and even relay-raced through the tricky tracks of digital etiquette and real-life conflicts. I hope you're feeling pumped with all the new tricks tucked into your social toolkit.

Let's do a quick victory lap around the core message of our time together: This book was all about empowering you—yes, you!—to navigate the wild world of social interactions with newfound confidence. From mastering the art of chitchat to building bridges of friendship that can withstand a bit of stormy weather, we've covered ground on improving communication, managing those stomach-churning anxious moments, and fostering a rock-solid sense of self-confidence.

Reflecting on our journey, it's clear that this wasn't just about picking up skills; it was a transformation. Each day, step by step, you've been equipped with the necessary tools not just to survive but thrive in your social universe. Whether it was handling rejection with grace or learning to listen like a pro, the growth you've experienced is designed to stick.

What are the takeaways? Remember, understanding who you are is your superpower when it comes to social interaction. Authenticity isn't just a buzzword; it's your secret weapon in making meaningful connections. Resilience, that tough cookie, will keep you going when the going gets tough. And never underestimate the power of empathy—it turns out, stepping into someone else's shoes is more than just a good stretch; it's a way to see the world in a whole new light.

On the note of individuality, let's not forget that your unique quirks and qualities aren't just extras; they're the main show. Embrace them. Rock them. Your individuality is what makes you not just part of the crowd but a standout star in it.

And hey, remember, mastering these social skills is not a 'one and done' deal. It's more like a video game; the more you play, the better you get. Keep practicing the strategies and exercises we've explored, and don't hesitate to revisit any section when you need a refresher.

Now, let's talk action! It's your turn to take these tools and start crafting your path. Improvement isn't just about know-ing; it's about doing. Step out of your comfort zone, strike up a conversation, and maybe even share what you've learned with a friend who could use a boost.

And speaking of sharing, why not share your journey? Hit up your socials, chat with your peers, or even start a blog. Your challenges, successes, and insights could light the way for others on similar paths and help build a community where everyone grows together.

Thank you, truly, for joining me on this adventure. It takes guts and gusto to dive into personal growth, and by turning the pages of this book, you've shown you have plenty of both. I'm grateful for your trust and commitment.

As we close this book (literally), remember that the skills you've gained are just the beginning. The road ahead is bright with promise, and I'm excited about the incredible social journeys you're destined to have. Here's to you—confidently communicating, building meaningful connections, and expressing your most authentic self. The world is way more fun with you fully in it. Keep shining, keep sharing, and let's make every interaction count!

MONEY SKILLS FOR TEENS MADE EASY: STEP-BY-STEP GUIDE TO FINANCIAL LITERACY, BASIC BUDGETING, AND SIMPLE SAVING FOR FINANCIAL INDEPENDENCE—EVEN IF YOU'RE JUST STARTING OUT

INTRODUCTION

"It's not about how much you have; it's about how you manage what you have."

WILL SMITH

Let me tell you about Jenna. She's sixteen and just got her first job. Thrilled with her newfound financial freedom, she splurged on the latest fashion and tech, only to find her wallet empty by month's end. A tale too familiar, right? Jenna's story is common. Many teens face similar challenges when it comes to managing their money. But here's the good news—understanding money doesn't have to be a mystery, and you can learn to handle it smartly.

Today's teens face a lot of financial challenges. Schools often skip over teaching money skills, leaving many of you clueless about budgeting or saving. There's also the constant peer pressure to buy the latest trends or gadgets, which makes saving even harder. And let's not forget the myths about money management that float around. Did you know that only about 24% of teens understand basic financial literacy concepts? Considering how essential these skills are for your future, that's a pretty low number.

This story highlights just how much we need a guide like this book, designed to make financial concepts clear and provide you with the savvy to manage your money wisely.

This is where this book comes in—a step-by-step guide through the journey of mastering money skills. You'll find practical tools and strategies to help you budget, save, and even start thinking about investing for your future. It's all about making these concepts easy and relatable so you can apply them immediately.

Let me share a bit about myself. I'm a parent of a teen and have always been passionate about helping teens like you. My journey began many years ago, and it's been rewarding. I've learned from financial experts, gained real-world experience, and seen firsthand how empowering it is when teens take control of their finances. Every lesson learned, and every hurdle overcome has been channeled into this book. Why? Because I'm enthusiastic about empowering all teens with the knowledge and tools for financial triumph.

So, what can you expect from this book? Well, by the time you finish reading, you'll know how to create and stick to a budget. You'll understand the basics of credit and how to use it wisely. And yes, we'll even touch on investing, so you'll have a head start on growing your money. The book aims to prepare you for financial independence, giving you the tools you need to make smart decisions with your money.

I'll use examples and language that resonate with you throughout the book. After all, I know that being a teen today comes with its own set of challenges and experiences. Whether it's navigating the latest trends or dealing with the pressure to spend, I've got your back. You're not alone in this journey, and I'm here to guide you every step of the way.

I also want you to engage with this book actively. Try the exercises, take the quizzes, and apply what you learn in real-life situations. This book isn't just about reading—it's about doing. And the more you practice, the more confident you'll become in managing your finances.

As you turn the pages, remember this: You have the power to shape your financial future. Financial literacy is within your reach, and it's a skill that will empower you for life. So, let's get started on this exciting journey to financial independence. You've got this!

SECTION 1: UNDERSTANDING THE BASICS OF MONEY MANAGEMENT

"The quicker you are to give away your money, the more likely you are to be poor."

J. COLE

Ever felt like your money just seems to disappear without a trace? You're not alone. I remember a time when a friend of mine, Alex, got his first paycheck. He was over the moon and spent it all on a new gaming console and a few nights out with friends. By the next week, he was flat broke, with no clue where all his money had gone. It's a familiar story, right? Many of us have been there, maybe not with a paycheck, but with birthday money or allowance. This section is about getting to grips with the basics of managing your money so it doesn't vanish into thin air.

We all face a bunch of challenges when it comes to money, especially as teens. Schools don't always teach us the ropes about personal finance. So, you might feel like you're tossed into the deep end when it comes to budgeting, saving, or understanding terms like "credit score." And let's not forget the pressure from friends to spend on the latest gear or social outings. It's easy to get swept up in the moment. But learning how to manage your money can help you avoid those "where did it all go?" moments and set you up for a financially savvy future.

~

MONEY TALK 101: BREAKING DOWN FINANCIAL JARGON

Let's dive into some of the financial terms you'll come across. Think of this as a quick guide to understanding money-speak. First up is "budget." Imagine it like planning out your week. Just as you'd allocate time for homework, hobbies, and hanging out, a budget is about dividing up your money for different needs and wants. It's all about balance. Next, there's "interest." Remember those video games where you can earn bonus points? Interest works similarly. When you save money, you earn a little extra as a reward. But when you borrow money, you pay a bit more back, which is the cost of borrowing. Easy, right?

Now, let's talk about "credit score." Credit score might sound complicated, but it's simply a number that shows how trust-worthy you are with borrowed money. It's like a report card for your finances. If you repay what you owe on time, your score stays high. But if you don't, it can drop. Lastly, there's the "savings account." Picture it as a secure vault where you stash your cash for future use, like saving up for a big purchase or a rainy day. It keeps your money safe and even helps it grow with interest.

Let's use a few more everyday comparisons to make these concepts stick. Think of "budgeting" like managing your time for homework and hobbies. You must make sure you're not spending all your time on one thing, or you'll fall behind in others. Similarly, if you overspend in one area, you might not have enough for the things you need. "Interest" can be likened to those loyalty points you earn at your favorite store. You get a little extra to keep your money with the bank or to pay off your credit card on time.

When it comes to digital tools, there are loads of apps and websites to help you get more familiar with these terms. Check out Investopedia for teens, It's like having a financial dictionary at your fingertips. Apps with glossaries are also super handy if you want to learn on the go. They can break down complex jargon into simpler terms, making it easier for you to understand and apply them in real life.

To help keep everything straight, a glossary of essential terms can be your best friend. This book includes a comprehensive list of terms that will pop up throughout your financial learning adventure. Think of it as your personal cheat sheet—perfect for those moments when a term slips your mind. Common acronyms and terms often mixed up will be there, ready for a quick refresh.

Understanding financial jargon is like learning a new language. It might seem tricky initially, but these terms will become familiar with practice. You'll soon see how they fit into your daily life, helping you make smarter decisions about your money. Remember, every expert was once a beginner, and with these tools, you'll be well on your way to financial fluency.

〜

WHY MONEY MATTERS: UNDERSTANDING THE ROLE OF FINANCE IN YOUR LIFE

Imagine waking up one day and deciding you want to travel, buy a new gadget, or even start a small business. What's the common thread in all these dreams? Money. It's no secret that money plays a massive role in our daily lives and future opportunities. The decisions you make now about spending versus saving can shape your future. If you spend every dollar you earn, you might find yourself stuck when that dream opportunity comes along.

On the other hand, saving a little bit every time you receive money can open doors you never thought possible. Financial literacy is more than just about saving for a rainy day; it's about paving a path toward the life you want to lead. Your financial habits today set the stage for your financial health tomorrow.

The beauty of gaining financial independence is the freedom it brings. You're in the driver's seat when you manage your own money. You get to decide what's important to you and prioritize your goals. Whether saving up for college, buying a car, or investing in your passion, having control over your finances lets you make personal decisions without relying on others. It's empowering to know that you can stand on your own two feet, financially speaking. This independence reduces the need to depend on parents or guardians and allows you to make choices that align with your values and aspirations.

But what happens if you ignore financial education? The consequences can be pretty challenging. Overspending is a common pitfall, where you might accumulate debt without realizing it. Credit cards, for example, can be a helpful tool but dangerous if misused. You could also miss out on opportunities to save or invest, which are crucial for building wealth over time. Without knowledge, you might find yourself in situations where financial decisions become overwhelming or intimidating. This lack of understanding can limit your ability to make informed choices, leaving you vulnerable to financial stress or crisis.

That's why it's important to take charge of your financial education. Be proactive about learning and take responsibility for your financial future. Engage in financial literacy programs that can provide structured learning and insights. Schwab Moneywise for instance, is a program that educates teens on budgeting, saving, and managing credit. It's about creating equal opportunities for financial freedom, regardless of your background. You can also seek mentorship from financially savvy individuals. These mentors can offer valuable advice and share experiences that help you confidently navigate your financial landscape.

Consider the impact of financial literacy on your life choices. When you understand money, you can make smarter decisions, from shopping to saving for big goals. You can weigh the pros and cons of a purchase or investment and decide what's truly worth your hard-earned cash. Financial literacy empowers you to see the bigger picture, helping you make strategic choices that benefit you in the long run. It's not just about having money; it's about making it work for you and supporting the life you envision.

Taking control of your finances begins with understanding the importance of managing money and recognizing its impact on your life. It's about acknowledging that financial literacy is a key ingredient in achieving the freedom to pursue your dreams and aspirations. By actively engaging in your financial education, you set yourself up for success and open up a world of possibilities. You become better equipped to handle financial challenges, seize opportunities, and create a future that aligns with your goals.

~

INCOME STREAMS: THE DIFFERENT WAYS TEENS CAN EARN MONEY

Imagine browsing through the latest sneakers at the mall and realizing you need a little extra cash. You're not alone in wanting to earn your own money, and the good news is that there are plenty of ways to do it. Let's explore some popular options. Part-time jobs are a classic choice, offering steady income and a taste of responsibility. Working in retail or food service pads your wallet and teaches valuable soft skills like customer service and teamwork. These roles can provide a sense of stability, with regular hours and a predictable paycheck, which can be a comforting introduction to the world of work.

On the flip side, freelancing might be for you if you crave flexibility and have a knack for creativity. Picture yourself as a graphic designer or writer, crafting your own schedule while earning money doing something you love. Freelancing lets you dive into projects that excite you, and you can often work from anywhere—your room, a café, or even the park. The freedom to pick and choose projects based on your interests and schedule is a significant perk. However, the freelance world can be unpredictable, with income that might fluctuate from month to month. You'll need to manage your time well to balance multiple clients or gigs.

Then there's the digital realm, where online platforms offer many opportunities. Tutoring, for instance, allows you to share your knowledge and help others while earning cash. Or consider providing digital services like social media management or video editing. These roles tap into your tech-savvy skills and let you work from the comfort of your home. They're perfect for teens already spending time online and wanting to monetize their skills. The challenge here is building a reputation and finding clients who trust your expertise, but the opportunities can be rewarding once you establish yourself.

Entrepreneurial spirits might find joy in starting a small business or side hustle. Whether it's selling handmade crafts or running a lawn care service, being your own boss lets you bring your ideas to life. It's all about identifying what you're passionate about and figuring out how to make it profitable. This path teaches you about marketing, customer relations, and financial management in real-time. But remember, running a business isn't all sunshine and rainbows. It requires commitment and resilience to weather slow sales periods or manage unexpected challenges.

Balancing work with school and leisure is crucial. You don't want to burn out or let your grades slip. It's important to set boundaries and prioritize your tasks. Think about how much time you can realistically dedicate to work without sacrificing your studies or downtime. Maybe you decide to work only on weekends or after school for a set number of hours. Maintaining a healthy balance ensures you excel in school while enjoying your earnings. Plus, it leaves room for relaxation, hobbies, and hanging out with friends. After all, life's not just about work—it's about enjoying your time and making the most of every opportunity.

Finding ways to earn money as a teen is more than just about the cash. It's about discovering what you enjoy, building confidence, and learning skills that will benefit you in the future. Each income stream offers its own set of challenges and rewards, and there's no one-size-fits-all. You might try one path and find it's not for you or discover a passion you never knew you had. The key is to stay curious, explore different avenues, and not be afraid to try something new. Earning money as a teen is your first step into a world of independence and possibility.

⌇

MONEY MYTHS BUSTED: DEBUNKING COMMON MISCONCEPTIONS

Ever heard someone say that saving is only for adults or that credit cards are nothing but trouble? These are just a couple of the myths floating around about money that can steer you off course. Let's start with saving. Some people think it's only something adults need to worry about, but that's far from the truth. Saving is crucial at any age. Imagine you want to buy something big, like a laptop, or even start saving for college. If you start saving now, even small amounts, it adds up over time. Plus, getting into the habit of saving early on sets you up for financial success in the future. It's not just about stashing cash away; it's about building a cushion for unexpected expenses or investing in your dreams.

Then there's the myth that credit cards are bad. Sure, if you misuse them, they can lead to debt, but credit cards can be beneficial when used responsibly. They help build your credit history, which is vital for things like renting an apartment or buying a car later on. Credit cards also offer rewards, like cash back or travel points, which you can use to your advantage. The key is to pay off your balance in full each month to avoid interest charges and debt accumulation. It's about being smart and disciplined with your spending. According to the article "7 Money Myths to Stop Believing Today," credit cards can offer purchase protection and help build credit history, making them more beneficial than debit cards in certain situations.

To counter these myths, let's look at some real-life examples. Take the story of Johnny, who started putting aside a small amount of money each month from his part-time job. Over time, that small amount grew, allowing him to invest in a business idea and further his education without taking on debt. There are countless stories of teens using credit cards wisely, earning rewards, and maintaining excellent credit scores, which opened doors to better financial opportunities.

Take Sarah, a high school senior who just turned 18. She decided to get her first credit card with a low credit limit of $500 to help build her credit score before going to college. Sarah was careful with her spending, only using her card for small, manageable purchases like gas and school supplies and always paying off the full balance every month. By using her card responsibly, Sarah started earning reward points that she could redeem for discounts at her favorite stores. More importantly, her consistent on-time payments helped her build an excellent credit score. Sarah had maintained a solid credit history by the time she graduated from college.

According to Experian, individuals with higher credit scores generally have access to lower interest rates on loans and better financial products, which can save thousands of dollars over a lifetime.

But it's not just about hearing stories. It's important to develop a habit of questioning the financial advice you hear. Not everything you read online or hear from friends is accurate. Think critically about the sources of your information. If a financial influencer recommends a product or investment, do some research. Check their credentials and see if facts back their advice. Be skeptical and ask questions. Are they credible? Is there a hidden agenda in their recommendations? Evaluating the credibility of financial advice is something that will benefit you well throughout your life.

A way to challenge these myths is by engaging in conversations about money. Talk to your family or friends about financial topics. Share what you've learned and listen to their perspectives. These conversations can be a great way to learn from each other and debunk myths together. Joining financial literacy clubs or groups can also provide a supportive environment to discuss and challenge financial misconceptions. These discussions help you gain new insights and reinforce the importance of making informed financial decisions.

Understanding these myths and learning to question them is a critical step in your financial education. It's not just about saving or using credit cards; it's about developing a mindset that values accurate information and responsible decision-making. By busting these myths, you empower yourself to take control of your financial future and make choices that align with your goals. Remember, the more informed you are, the better you'll be able to navigate the financial world confidently and clearly.

~

FINANCIAL GOALS: SETTING AND ACHIEVING MONEY MILESTONES

Setting financial goals is like plotting a course on a map. You need to know where you're headed to figure out how to get there. Imagine wanting to buy a new phone or save for a big trip—these are your destinations. But how do you reach them? That's where SMART goals come into play. SMART stands for Specific, Measurable, Achievable, Relevant, and Time-bound. Let's break that down. Being specific means you decide exactly what you want. Instead of just saying, "I want to save money," you say, "I want to save $1,000 for a new phone." Measurable is about keeping track, like knowing you've saved $100 out of that $1,000. Achievable asks, is this realistic? If you earn $50 a week, saving $1,000 in two months might be a stretch, but in nine months, it's doable. Relevant checks if this goal makes sense with your overall plans, and time-bound gives you a deadline, like saving by your birthday.

Once your goals are set, staying motivated is critical. Remember, it's a marathon, not a sprint. Tracking your progress can help keep you on track and fired up. You might use a simple app to log each contribution to your savings or a spreadsheet to see how close you are to your target. Every penny saved is a step closer to your goal, and that's some-thing to celebrate. Whether treating yourself to a small reward when you hit a milestone or sharing your progress with friends or family, these moments of recognition can fuel your determination.

You'll want some handy tools and strategies in your back pocket to reach your goals. Budgeting apps are fantastic for tracking income and expenses, helping you see where you can cut back to save more. They're like a personal coach, guiding you toward your financial objectives. Another great method is creating vision boards. These are visual representations of your goals—pictures, words, or anything that inspires you to keep pushing forward. Place it somewhere you'll see often, like a wall in your room. It serves as a daily reminder of what you're working towards and why it matters.

Life isn't static, and neither are our goals. Sometimes, what we want changes, or unexpected events require us to shift our priorities. That's why it's important to reflect on your goals periodically. Maybe you've decided that instead of a new phone, you'd rather save for a summer course that aligns with your passion. Or perhaps a setback has occurred, like an unexpected expense, and you need to adjust your timeline. Being flexible and willing to adapt ensures that your goals remain relevant to your life. Learning from setbacks is crucial, too. Each challenge is an opportunity to understand how you can improve and avoid similar issues in the future.

Setting financial goals isn't just about the end result. It's about building a mindset that values planning, persistence, and adaptability. These skills will serve you well beyond achieving one particular goal. They lay the foundation for making informed financial decisions throughout your life. As you practice setting and achieving these goals, you'll find a sense of accomplishment and confidence that comes from taking control of your financial path. Remember, it's not just about having money—it's about using it to create the life you envision. By setting clear goals and working diligently towards them, you take decisive steps toward a future filled with possibilities.

Activity: Build Your Budget

Objective: To help you understand the concept of budgeting and apply it to your everyday life.

Step 1: Identify Your Income: List any weekly or monthly income you receive, such as allowance, part-time job earnings, or money from chores.

Example:
- Allowance: $20/week
- Babysitting: $15/week

Step 2: Categorize Your Spending: Break your spending into categories like food, entertainment, savings, etc. Estimate how much you typically spend in each category.

Example:
- Entertainment: $15/week
- Food: $10/week
- Savings: $10/week

Step 3: Create Your Budget: Create a simple budget based on your income and spending habits. Adjust your spending so that you have some money left over for savings.

Example Budget:
- Entertainment: $10/week
- Food: $10/week
- Savings: $15/week

Step 4: Track Your Spending: Track your real spending for one week and compare it to your budget. Did you stick to your budget? If not, how can you adjust?

Step 5: Reflect: Reflect on your budgeting experience. Were there any surprises? What changes would you make to your budget going forward?

Quiz: Money Talk 101 - Test Your Knowledge

1. What is a budget?
   a. A list of things you want to buy.
   b. A plan for how you spend and save your money.
   c. A loan you take out from a bank.
2. What is interest?
   a. Money you pay when you borrow money.
   b. A reward you earn when you save money.
   c. Both a and b.
3. What is a credit score?
   a. A number that shows how much money you have saved.
   b. A score that tells how trustworthy you are when borrowing money.
   c. A report card from your bank.
4. Which of the following is the best way to describe a savings account?
   a. A place to stash money for future use.
   b. An account where you borrow money.
   c. A place to spend money on big purchases.
5. Which of the following is NOT a financial term?
   a. Credit score
   b. Interest
   c. PlayStation

Answer Key:

1. b) A plan for how you spend and save your money.
2. c) Both a and b.
3. b) A score that tells how trustworthy you are when borrowing money.
4. a) A place to stash money for future use.
5. c) PlayStation

Our journey begins at Base Camp, where we gather essential tools to understand income, expenses, and the value of money.

SECTION 2: BUDGETING ESSENTIALS FOR TEENS

"It's not about having a lot of money. It's knowing how to manage it."

T-PAIN

I magine this: you've just received your birthday money, and your first thought is to spend it all on that new game or those trendy shoes everyone's been talking about. But what if there was a way to make that money stretch further, to help you not just buy what you want now but also save for something even bigger down the line? This is where budgeting comes in. It's your financial roadmap, guiding you on how to spend your money wisely while keeping your long-term goals in sight. Think of it as Google Maps for your finances, helping you navigate from where you are now to where you want to be.

Budgeting is crucial because it aligns your spending with your priorities. Without a budget, losing track of where your money goes is easy. You might find yourself asking, "Why don't I have any money left?" A budget helps you avoid this by setting clear guidelines for your spending. It's about deciding what's most important to you and making sure your money supports those choices. Whether saving for a concert, a new skateboard, or even college, a budget ensures you're not spending on impulse but working towards something meaningful.

Setting up a budget doesn't have to be complicated. Start by listing all the ways you earn money, whether it's from a part-time job, allowance, or even gifts from relatives. Next, think about your expenses. Break them down into two categories: needs and wants. "Needs" are things you absolutely have to pay for, like your phone bill or bus fare. "Wants" are those nice-to-have items, like a new pair of jeans or a night out with friends. This separation is key because it helps you see where you can cut back if necessary.

Once you have your income and expenses laid out, it's time to do some simple math. Subtract your expenses from your income if you have money left over. That's great! You can save it or decide on a want you can afford. If you're in the negative, it's time to reevaluate. Maybe cut back on some of those wants or look for ways to increase your income, like picking up an extra shift at work. This exercise is all about balance and ensuring you're not spending more than you earn, which is the essence of budgeting.

Sticking to a budget requires discipline. It's about having the self-control to say no to things that aren't in your budget, even if they're tempting. Budgeting doesn't mean you can't have fun; it just means being smart about it. For instance, if your friends are going out to eat but you're watching your spending, suggest a budget-friendly alternative like a potluck at someone's house. It's these small decisions that help you stay on track. Commitment and self-control are your allies in making sure your budget works for you, not against you.

Flexibility is also important in budgeting. Life is unpredictable, and sometimes your budget needs to adjust. That's why regular check-ins are crucial. At the end of each month, review your budget. Look at what worked and what didn't. Maybe you spent less on transportation than you thought or more on snacks. Use this information to tweak your budget for the next month. This way, it stays relevant and reflects your actual spending habits and needs.

Budgeting Exercise: Craft Your First Budget

Grab a notebook or open a spreadsheet. List all your sources of income in one column. In another column, write down your expenses, separating needs from wants. Calculate the difference between your income and expenses. Think about your financial goals —what can you save for? Adjust your spending plan to make room for these goals. Review it at the end of the month and adjust where needed. These reviews are your first step to financial independence.

Income source	Amount	Expenses				Difference Amount
		Needs	Amount	Wants	Amount	
Birthday blessings money	$$	Phone bill	$$	Playstation	$$	$$
Total	~~~	~~~	~~~	~~~	~~~	~~~

Budgeting might sound like a lot of work, but it's a skill that pays off in more ways than one. It gives you control over your money, helps you make informed decisions, and sets you up for future financial success. Once you get the hang of it, budgeting becomes second nature, a part of your routine that guides you toward your goals. Whether saving for something special or just keeping track of your cash, a budget is your best friend on the road to financial freedom.

THE 50/30/20 RULE: SIMPLIFYING BUDGETING FOR TEENS

Imagine you've just got your hands on your allowance or your paycheck from a part-time gig. The temptation to splurge on a concert ticket is real, right? But what if you could spend, save, and still have fun without losing track? That's where the 50/30/20 rule comes into play. This rule is like a friendly guide, helping you divvy up your money in a way that makes sense. It's simple: 50% of your income goes to needs—think essentials like your phone bill or gas. Another 30% is for wants, the fun stuff like a movie night or eating out. The remaining 20%? That's your savings, whether for an emergency fund or future goals like a new laptop. This approach keeps things straightforward, making budgeting easier without feeling overwhelmed.

The beauty of the 50/30/20 rule is its flexibility. It acknowledges that not everyone's financial situation is the same. For instance, if your income is on the lower side, you might need to tweak those percentages a bit. Perhaps you allocate 60% to needs and tighten the belt on wants, making it 20% while still keeping 20% for savings. Conversely, if you're lucky enough to have a bit more cash coming in, you might find you can comfortably stick to the original breakdown—or even save a bit more. The key is adjusting the rule to fit your life so it feels natural and not like a financial straitjacket.

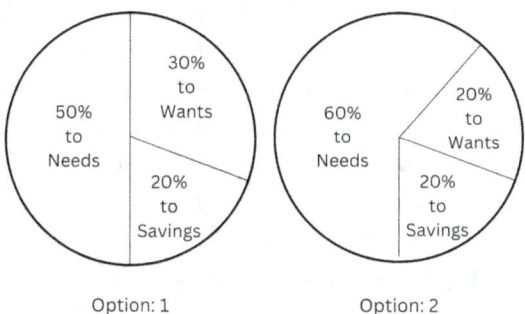

Option: 1   Option: 2

How does this rule look in action? Let's say you receive $200 a month. According to the 50/30/20 guideline, $100 would cover your needs—maybe that's your contribution to the family grocery bill or your monthly data plan. You then have $60 for wants, allowing you a couple of dinners out or that new video game. Lastly, $40 goes straight into savings. It might not seem like much at first, but those savings add up over time, setting you up for the bigger things you're eyeing in the future. This method helps ensure that you're not just spending everything at once but making thoughtful choices about where your money goes.

One of the biggest perks of using the 50/30/20 rule is how it reduces financial stress. Having clear categories for your money means you don't have to constantly worry about whether you're overspending or if you'll have enough for next month. You know that your needs are covered, your wants are manageable, and you're actively saving for what's next. It's a balanced approach that takes the guesswork out of budgeting, allowing you to make decisions confidently. When you follow this rule, you're not just spending mindlessly—you're making your money work for you in a way that's both practical and empowering.

Consider creating a simple chart or using a budgeting app to help you visualize how this rule can fit into your life. List your monthly income at the top, then break it down into three categories. Write out what you expect to spend in each category and track it throughout the month, which can be a fun exercise that can keep you on track and give you a sense of accomplishment as you see your savings grow and your spending stays within limits. Whether you're saving for something big or just trying to get a handle on your daily expenses, the 50/30/20 rule offers a solid foundation that's easy to understand and apply.

Budgeting doesn't have to be a chore. With the 50/30/20 rule, you have a simple, flexible method to manage your money that respects your individuality and financial circumstances. It's about finding balance, reducing stress, and setting yourself up for success, all while keeping things straightforward. Whether you're just starting out or looking to refine your budgeting skills, this rule offers a practical approach that can make managing your finances feel less like a burden and more like a natural part of your everyday life.

∽

TRACKING YOUR SPENDING: TOOLS AND APPS TO STAY ON TOP

Picture this: it's the end of the month, and you're scratching your head, trying to figure out where all your money went. You know you've had enough of that new game, but somehow, it slipped through your fingers, which is why tracking your expenses is crucial. It's like having a magnifying glass on your spending habits, helping you see exactly where your money goes and revealing patterns you might not have noticed. Maybe you didn't realize how much those daily coffee runs add up or how those small online purchases can sneak up on you. Tracking your spending gives you a clear picture, enabling you to make more informed decisions and adjust your habits accordingly.

In today's digital age, you've got a whole arsenal of tools at your disposal to help track your expenses. Apps like Mint and YNAB (You Need A Budget) are popular choices for a reason. Mint connects to your bank accounts and automatically categorizes your spending, giving you a visual dashboard of where your money is going. YNAB, on the other hand, encourages you to plan for every dollar you earn, making it a proactive approach to budgeting. If you prefer a more hands-on method, spreadsheets can be a great tool, allowing you to manually enter your expenses and customize categories to fit your needs. These tools are designed to make tracking your spending as easy as possible so you can focus on what really matters—making your money work for you.

Choosing the right tool is all about finding what fits your style and needs. If you're always on the go, an app that syncs across devices might be your best bet. Look for user-friendly interfaces that don't overwhelm you with too many features. You want something intuitive that doesn't require a finance degree to use. Compatibility is another key factor. Make sure the tool works with your devices, whether that's an iPhone, Android, or desktop computer. Some people thrive with colorful charts and graphs, while others prefer straightforward lists and numbers. Try a couple of different options and see which one feels most natural to you.

Once you've set up your tool, the real magic happens when you start reviewing your tracked expenses regularly. Think of it like a monthly check-up for your finances; it is your chance to analyze your data and see what's working and what's not. Maybe you're spending more on takeout than you thought, or perhaps you're underspending on essentials like groceries. Use this insight to tweak your budget and set new goals. Perhaps you can cut back on one area to save more for something you really want. The point is to learn from your spending habits, not just record them.

Over time, you'll start to see patterns in your spending. Identifying these patterns is a game-changer. You'll understand where you might be leaking money and where you have room to save. This awareness is empowering. It helps you make smarter choices and feel more in control of your finances. You might discover that a small change, like brewing your own coffee every day instead of buying it, can free up funds for something bigger and more exciting.

Interactive Exercise: Monthly Expense Report

At the end of each month, take a few minutes to create your expense report. Use your chosen tool to categorize all your spending. Look for areas where you spent more or less than expected. Ask yourself why these differences occurred, and think about how you can adjust for the next month. This practice not only keeps you accountable but also makes budgeting a regular part of your routine.

Tracking your spending might seem tedious at first, but it's a habit that pays off. It brings a sense of clarity and confidence to your financial life. With the right tools, it becomes less of a chore and more of an insightful practice. You'll find yourself making better choices with your money, reducing stress, and feeling more prepared for whatever financial challenges come your way.

~

DEALING WITH UNEXPECTED EXPENSES: BUILDING FLEXIBILITY INTO YOUR BUDGET

Life has a funny way of throwing us curveballs when we least expect them, and finances are no different. This has happened to all of us; you're riding your bike home, and suddenly, the chain snaps. Or maybe you're texting away when your phone screen shatters. These kinds of unexpected expenses can pop up out of nowhere, hitting your wallet hard if you're not prepared. It's not just emergencies, either. Think about those last-minute party invites or spontaneous plans with friends. While they're fun, they can quickly derail your financial plans if you haven't planned for them. Having a strategy for these surprises is key to keeping your budget in check and avoiding the stress of scrambling for cash at the last minute.

One of the best ways to handle these surprises is by creating a small emergency fund. Think of it as a financial safety net for life's unplanned moments. It adds up over time, even if you just put aside a little bit from each paycheck or allowance. This fund can be a lifesaver when you need to cover those unexpected costs without dipping into money meant for other things. Another smart move is to allocate a buffer amount in your budget, specifically for those just-in-case moments. It's like having a cushion that absorbs the financial shock, allowing you to deal with surprises without throwing your entire budget out of whack.

Savings play a crucial role in managing unforeseen costs. They act as your financial backup, ready to jump in when life catches you off guard. Without savings, you might find yourself reaching for a credit card or borrowing money, which can lead to debt and more stress. But with some planning and discipline, your savings can cover these costs, keeping your financial health intact. It's about having peace of mind, knowing that you've got a plan in place for whatever comes your way. This safety net is not just about avoiding debt; it's about making sure you're free to focus on the important things in life rather than worrying about money.

Proactive financial planning is your ally in this battle against unexpected expenses. Anticipating and preparing for uncertainties can make all the difference. Take seasonal expenses, for instance. School supplies, holiday gifts, or even a summer trip—all these can sneak up on you if you're not careful. When you plan ahead and set aside a little each month, you ensure these costs don't catch you by surprise. Anticipating these expenses allows you to spread the cost over time, making it easier to manage when the time comes. This foresight helps you avoid the last-minute scramble and ensures you stay financially stable throughout the year.

To make this work, you must be honest about what might come up and when. Think about your year and any events or needs that might arise. Once you've identified these potential surprises, incorporate them into your budget. Even if it's just a rough estimate, having a plan gives you a structure to work with. This way, when something unexpected does happen, you're not thrown off course. Instead, you can adjust your budget as needed, feeling confident that you've prepared for the unexpected.

Reflection Exercise: Identifying Potential Surprises

Take a moment to reflect on your life and identify any potential financial surprises. Think about past experiences, upcoming events, or even things you've read about. Write them down and consider how they might affect your finances. Use this list to create a plan for handling these costs, whether through an emergency fund, a budget buffer, or proactive savings. This exercise helps you stay ahead of the game, ensuring you're ready for whatever life throws your way.

Building flexibility into your budget isn't just about avoiding financial trouble. It's about creating a sense of security and control over your money, allowing you to focus on what truly matters. Whether it's an emergency repair, a surprise party, or a seasonal expense, being prepared means you can handle it all confidently and easily. This approach not only protects your financial health but also empowers you to enjoy life's unexpected moments without the worry of financial strain.

～

BUDGETING WITH FRIENDS: MANAGING SOCIAL PRESSURES

Think about a time you're out with your friends, and they decide to hit up that new burger place everyone's been raving about. Suddenly, you're faced with a dilemma: stick to your budget or join in on the fun. Social dynamics can significantly impact how we handle our money. Peer pressure often tempts us to stretch our wallets further than we should. It's tough to say no when everyone else seems to be spending without care. But staying true to your financial goals doesn't mean you have to miss out on social events. It's about finding a balance that lets you enjoy time with friends without wrecking your budget.

One way to maintain discipline in social settings is by suggesting budget-friendly activities. Instead of dining out, why not propose a picnic at the park or a movie night at home? These alternatives are not only easier on your wallet but can also be more memorable and fun. Setting spending limits ahead of time can also help. Before heading out, decide how much you're comfortable spending and stick to it. Let your friends know your budget constraints so they understand your decisions. Most of the time, they'll respect your boundaries and might even appreciate the reminder to be mindful of their own spending.

Having open discussions about money with your friends can make a huge difference. Share your budgeting tips and experiences, and encourage them to do the same. Maybe you've found a way to save on streaming services, or they've discovered a new app that tracks expenses. These conversations not only help you learn from each other but also build a culture of transparency and understanding. You'll find that many of your friends might be dealing with similar financial pressures, and talking about it can relieve some of the stress. It's about creating an environment where money isn't a taboo topic but something you can openly discuss and manage together.

Group accountability can also be a powerful tool in achieving financial goals. Consider creating a shared savings challenge with your friends. Perhaps you all set a goal to save a certain amount by the end of the month or plan a group outing that requires everyone to save up for it. This shared commitment fosters a sense of teamwork and motivates everyone to stay on track. It's like having a built-in support system where you cheer each other on and celebrate milestones together. Plus, it turns saving money into a fun and engaging activity rather than a solitary chore.

Reflection Exercise: Budget Buddies

Think about forming a "budget buddy" group with your friends. Meet regularly to discuss your financial goals and share progress. Use these meetings to plan budget-friendly activities and support each other in sticking to your budgets. This exercise not only strengthens your friendships but also helps you stay accountable and motivated.

Navigating social pressures is all about finding ways to blend your financial goals with your social life. It's not about depriving yourself of fun but making sure that fun doesn't derail your financial plans. You can enjoy the best of both worlds by being open about your budget, suggesting cost-effective alternatives, and leaning on your friends for support. Remember, true friends respect your financial boundaries and will likely appreciate your efforts to keep things affordable. So next time you're faced with a spending decision, take a moment to consider your goals, communicate with your friends, and make a choice that aligns with both.

Quiz: Budgeting Essentials

1. What's the first thing you should do when setting up a budget?
   a. Write down all your expenses.
   b. Decide what you want to buy.
   c. List all the ways you earn money.
   d. Plan your next shopping trip.
2. If you earn $100 a month and want to follow the 50/30/20 rule, how much should you ideally save?
   a. $50
   b. $30
   c. $20
   d. $10

3. What's the difference between "needs" and "wants"?
   a. Needs are things you really want, and wants are things you can do without.
   b. Needs are essential expenses like transportation and phone bills, while wants are fun but non-essential items like video games or new clothes.
   c. Wants are things your friends buy, and needs are things you like.
   d. Needs are things you want now, and wants are things you want later.

4. If your friends invite you to an expensive dinner, but you're trying to stick to your budget, what's a smart alternative?
   a. Tell them you'll join and put it on your credit card.
   b. Suggest a budget-friendly potluck or movie night at home.
   c. Go to the dinner but skip your next meal to save money.
   d. Ignore your budget this time because it's a special occasion.

5. Why is it important to review your budget at the end of each month?
   a. To make sure you still have enough money for video games.
   b. Adjust your budget based on how much you actually spent and plan for the next month.
   c. To see if you can cut out more "needs."
   d. To decide which friends to invite for the next expensive outing.

6. True or False: Sticking to a budget means you can't have any fun.
   a. True
   b. False

7. What is the 50/30/20 rule?
   a. 50% for wants, 30% for needs, 20% for savings.
   b. 50% for needs, 30% for wants, 20% for savings.
   c. 50% for fun, 30% for snacks, 20% for nothing.
   d. 50% for spending, 30% for fun, 20% for borrowing.

8. If you find that you're consistently going over your budget, what should you do?
   a. Borrow money from friends to cover the difference.
   b. Cut back on non-essential "wants" or find ways to increase your income.
   c. Use your credit card for the extra expenses.
   d. Ignore the budget; it's probably just a suggestion anyway.

9. Which of the following tools can help you track your spending?
   a. A spreadsheet
   b. Budgeting apps like Mint or YNAB
   c. Writing everything down in a notebook
   d. All of the above

10. Why is flexibility important when budgeting?
   a. So you can change your mind about how much to spend whenever you want.
   b. Because life is unpredictable, and sometimes unexpected expenses pop up.
   c. It's not important—budgets should never change.
   d. To allow for unlimited spending on fun things.

Answer Key:

1. c) List all the ways you earn money.
2. c) $20

3. b) Needs are essential expenses like transportation and phone bills, while wants are fun but non-essential items like video games or new clothes.

4. b) Suggest a budget-friendly potluck or movie night at home.

5. b) Adjust your budget based on how much you actually spent and plan for the next month.

6. b) False. You can still have fun, but budgeting helps you plan your spending and make smarter choices about where your money goes.

7. b) 50% for needs, 30% for wants, 20% for savings.

8. b) Cut back on non-essential "wants" or find ways to increase your income.

9. d) All of the above

10. b) Because life is unpredictable, and sometimes unexpected expenses pop up.

As we wrap up this Section, remember the power of managing your money with intention and awareness, even amidst social influences. The journey to financial independence is about balancing enjoyment with responsibility, and each step you take strengthens your financial foundation. Next, we'll explore how understanding credit can further empower you on this path.

Navigating through Budgeting Bay, we chart our course, carefully balancing our 'Wants' and 'Needs' to stay on track.

SECTION 3: THE ART OF SAVING

"A penny saved is a penny earned."

BENJAMIN FRANKLIN

I magine this: you're at your favorite store, eyeing that sleek new phone that just came out. The one with the amazing camera and all the cool features your current one lacks. The price tag is steep, and your wallet isn't exactly bursting with cash, and where saving comes into play. Saving money is like planting a seed that will eventually grow into something beautiful and valuable. It's about making choices today that will pay off in the future, whether it's for something you want next month or a few years down the road. In this Section, we'll explore how to set and achieve savings goals that align with your dreams, both big and small.

Let's start by distinguishing between short-term and long-term financial goals. Short-term goals are those things you want to achieve in the near future, usually within a year. Think about saving for a concert ticket, a new video game, or even a stylish jacket for the upcoming winter. These goals are usually more immediate and can be exciting because the payoff is just around the corner. On the other hand, long-term goals are your big-picture dreams, like saving for college tuition or buying your first car. These might take several years to accomplish, but the satisfaction you'll feel when you achieve them is worth the wait. Categorizing your goals helps you prioritize and allocate your resources accordingly, ensuring you're saving blindly and purposefully.

Setting achievable savings targets is crucial in making your goals a reality and where the SMART criteria come into play. SMART stands for Specific, Measurable, Achievable, Relevant, and Time-bound. For example, instead of saying, "I want to save money," a SMART goal would be, "I want to save $300 for a new computer by the end of the summer." This goal is specific because it clearly states what you want and is measurable because you can track your progress toward $300. It's achievable if you plan to save a certain amount each week, which is relevant because it aligns with your desire to upgrade your computer and is time-bound with a clear deadline. Using SMART criteria provides a framework that can help you define clear and realistic savings objectives, making them less daunting and more attainable.

Regular assessment of your savings progress is essential to ensure your goals remain on track. Life can be unpredictable, and your financial situation might change. Perhaps you will get a part-time job, or maybe your expenses will increase. Regularly checking in on your progress allows you to adjust your plan as needed. Maybe you find that you're able to save more than expected, or perhaps you need to extend your timeline. These adjustments ensure that your goals are always relevant and within reach. Regular reviews also motivate you by showing how far you've come and what's left to achieve. It's like having a financial checkpoint that aligns you with your aspirations.

One of the benefits of visualizing your goals is that it keeps them at the forefront of your mind. Using tools like goal trackers or vision boards can be incredibly motivating. A goal tracker might be an app that helps you set milestones and alerts you when you hit them. Imagine the satisfaction of seeing a progress bar inch closer to your target each week. Vision boards, on the other hand, are more creative. You can fill them with images and words representing your goals, like a picture of the college you want to attend or the car you dream of driving. Place it somewhere visible, like on your wall or as your phone wallpaper. These visual reminders keep you focused and inspired, acting as a constant nudge toward your success.

Interactive Tool: Goal Tracker Apps

Consider using apps like Greenlight or Copper Banking, which offer goal-setting features and financial education tailored for teens. These apps can help you monitor your savings, set reminders, and even provide financial tips to keep you motivated. Experiment with different apps to find one that suits your style and needs. This interactivity makes saving an engaging and rewarding experience, helping you stay committed to your goals.

By categorizing your goals, setting SMART targets, and regularly assessing your progress, you lay a strong foundation for successful saving. Remember, saving is a journey, and every small step counts. With the right mindset and tools, you can turn your financial dreams into reality, whether they're just around the corner or years in the making.

~

THE MAGIC OF COMPOUND INTEREST: HOW YOUR MONEY GROWS

Think of compound interest as a snowball rolling down a hill. At first, it starts small, just a little clump of snow. But as it keeps rolling, it picks up more snow, growing larger and larger. That's how compound interest works with your money. It's not just about earning interest on your initial savings but also on the interest accumulating over time. Your money can grow exponentially, especially if you start saving early. It's like having your money work for you, earning more money as it sits in your account. The magic happens when you let it sit long enough to keep building on itself.

To see how powerful compounding can be, consider this example: Imagine you saved $1,000 at a 5% annual interest rate. With simple interest, you'd earn $50 each year, totaling $1,500 after ten years. But with compound interest, you earn interest on your growing balance. By the end of ten years, your initial $1,000 would grow to about $1,628. That's an extra $128 without lifting a finger, all thanks to compounding. The difference might not seem huge initially, but multiply that over decades, and it becomes significant. This is why compounding is often called the "eighth wonder of the world" in finance. It's the secret sauce to growing your savings faster and more efficiently than traditional methods.

Saving early is critical to maximizing the benefits of compound interest. The earlier you begin, the more time your money has to grow. Imagine two friends, Alex and Jamie. Alex starts saving $100 a month at age 15, while Jamie waits until 25 to do the same. By the time they both reach 35, Alex's savings will have grown significantly more, even though they both saved the same amount each month. The difference? Alex gave compound interest more time to work its magic. By starting saving early, you are giving your savings a head start, allowing even small contributions to grow into sizable amounts over time. It's like planting a tree; the sooner you plant it, the sooner it can grow tall and strong.

To leverage compound interest effectively, look for savings accounts that offer compounding features. Many banks provide accounts that compound interest monthly or even daily, which can significantly boost your savings. It's worth shopping around to find the best rates and compounding frequencies. Another strategy is to make regular contributions to your account, even if they're small, keep your balance growing, and allow compounding to work on a more significant sum. Consistency is your friend here. The more consistently you save, the more opportunities you give your money to benefit from compounding. It's like feeding a growing plant; regular watering helps it flourish.

Also, consider automating your savings. By setting up automatic transfers from your checking account to your savings account, you're consistently adding to your savings without even thinking about it. It's a hands-off approach that ensures you're always contributing, maximizing the potential for compound interest. Some banks and apps even allow you to round up purchases to the nearest dollar, depositing the spare change into your savings. These small amounts add up over time, further boosting your balance and the compounding effect. Automation can be a game-changer, especially if you find it hard to remember to save regularly.

Understanding and utilizing compound interest can transform your financial future. By starting early, choosing the right accounts, and making regular contributions, you can watch your savings grow exponentially. It's about being smart with your decisions and letting time do the heavy lifting. Compound interest isn't just a financial concept; it's a tool that, when used wisely, can provide security and freedom in the years to come. So, why not let your money work for you and see where the magic of compounding can take you?

~

DIGITAL PIGGY BANKS: BEST APPS FOR TEEN SAVERS

In today's tech-savvy world, saving money has never been easier, thanks to a range of digital tools designed with you in mind. Imagine having a personal assistant that not only tracks your savings but also helps you grow them without much effort. That's what these apps do. Take Acorns, for instance. It's perfect for micro-investing. Every time you make a purchase, Acorns rounds up the amount to the nearest dollar and invests the spare change. It's like saving money without even realizing it, using those small amounts to build a more significant financial picture over time. Then there's Oportun, which takes a different approach. It analyzes your spending habits and automatically saves a little bit here and there, moving it into a savings account. You set your preferences, and Oportun does the heavy lifting, ensuring you're saving regularly without having to think about it.

The beauty of these digital tools lies in their ability to simplify and enhance the saving process. They make saving money fun and engaging. With features like automatic transfers, you can set up your app to move a certain amount of money into savings at regular intervals, like every payday. The "set it and forget it" method ensures you're consistently contributing to your savings goals. Many of these apps also come with goal-setting features, allowing you to outline what you're saving for, whether a new laptop or a college fund. As you save, the app tracks your progress, giving you visual updates that are both satisfying and motivating. You see your savings grow bit by bit, making the whole process rewarding and encouraging you to stick with it.

Choosing the right app depends mainly on your personal needs and preferences. When evaluating apps, consider the user interface: Is it easy to navigate? Does it look appealing to you? An app that's intuitive and visually engaging makes the experience more enjoyable. Another important factor is how well the app integrates with your existing bank accounts. Seamless integration means you spend less time fiddling with settings and more time focusing on your savings. Some apps also offer educational resources, teaching you about financial literacy as you save. If learning while saving appeals to you, look for apps that provide these benefits. Ultimately, the best app is one that fits your financial habits and lifestyle, making saving a natural part of your daily routine.

Don't hesitate to experiment with different apps to find the one that suits you best. Many of these tools offer free trials, allowing you to test their features before committing. Try a few and see which feels most comfortable. You might find that one app's style resonates more with your approach to saving or that another offers features you didn't know you needed. This trial-and-error process is valuable; it helps you explore options and learn more about what works for you. Personal finance is not a one-size-fits-all solution, and having the flexibility to tailor your tools to your needs is empowering.

Try It Out: Explore Saving Apps

Take advantage of free trials to explore different saving apps. Download Acorns or Oportun and spend a week familiarizing yourself with their features. Pay attention to how easy they are to use and how well they fit your saving habits. This hands-on approach will help you decide which app best supports your financial goals, making saving money an enjoyable and effortless part of your life.

Embracing technology in your savings journey can transform how you manage money. Selecting the right digital tools simplifies the process, making it more accessible and less daunting. Whether through automated savings, progress tracking, or goal setting, these apps provide a modern approach to managing your finances. They keep you engaged and motivated, ensuring that saving money is not just a chore but an

exciting step towards achieving your financial dreams.

~

EMERGENCY FUNDS: PREPARING FOR LIFE'S SURPRISES

Imagine this: you're cruising through life, feeling good about your finances, and then—bam!—your laptop crashes right before finals, or you suddenly need to see a doctor. Life is full of surprises, some of which can hit your wallet hard, and where having an emergency fund comes in handy. An emergency fund is like a financial cushion, softening the blow of unexpected expenses. It's a stash of cash set aside specifically for those "just in case" moments. Whether it's covering sudden medical bills, fixing a broken phone, or dealing with urgent repairs, having this financial safety net means you won't have to rely on credit cards or loans that could lead to debt. It's about having peace of mind, knowing you're prepared for whatever life throws your way.

Now, you might be wondering how much you should aim to save in your emergency fund. A common rule of thumb is to save enough to cover three to six months' worth of living expenses. But let's break that down into something more manageable for you. Start by saving a certain percentage of your monthly income—say 10% or whatever feels doable. If you're earning a part-time wage or getting an allowance, even setting aside a small amount each month can make a big difference. The key is consistency. Over time, those small contributions grow into a solid financial buffer. Adjust the percentage based on your comfort level and financial situation. The goal is to build a fund that feels right for you, providing security without stretching your finances too thin.

Building an emergency fund doesn't have to feel overwhelming. Start small and build gradually. Consider allocating a portion of each paycheck or any money you receive, like birthday gifts. Maybe you get a bonus for doing well at work or a surprise check from a relative—redirect those toward your emergency fund. It's about making saving a habit, turning it into a regular part of your financial routine. You might find that you can save more in some months, and in others, you can save less. That's okay. The important thing is to keep going, even if it's just a little at a time. Every dollar you save is a step closer to financial security.

Maintaining your emergency fund is just as important as building it. Once you dip into it for an emergency, make a plan to replenish it as soon as you can. Regular contributions help keep the fund intact and ready for whenever you need it again. Think of it as a cycle—use, replenish, repeat. This way, you're always prepared, no matter what. It's about creating a sustainable system that supports you through life's ups and downs. You might even want to set a reminder to review your fund every few months, ensuring it stays aligned with your needs and goals.

Consider this approach: automate your savings. Set up automatic transfers from your checking account to your emergency fund. This way, you're paying yourself first, ensuring your fund grows without you having to think about it. Automation takes the guesswork out of saving, making it easy to stay on track. It's a simple yet effective strategy that ensures your emergency fund is always a priority. Plus, it reduces the temptation to spend the money elsewhere, keeping your savings goal front and center.

Having an emergency fund gives you the confidence to face unexpected expenses head-on. It's about taking control of your financial future, ensuring you're ready for what life throws your way. With a solid emergency fund in place, you can move forward with peace of mind, knowing you've got the resources to handle whatever comes next. This financial cushion isn't just about money; it's about security, freedom, and the ability to navigate life's surprises with ease and grace.

～

SAVING HACKS: CREATIVE WAYS TO MAXIMIZE YOUR SAVINGS

Picture this: every time you buy a coffee or a snack, you're also tucking away a little bit of change into your savings. Sounds effortless, right? This is the magic of round-up savings. Many banks and apps offer a feature that rounds up your purchases to the nearest dollar and deposits the difference into your savings account. It's like saving money without feeling the pinch. Over time, these small amounts add up, turning spare change into a substantial sum. It's an easy and effective way to boost your savings without changing your spending habits drastically.

Another smart hack is taking advantage of cashback rewards. These are incentives offered by credit card companies or shopping apps that give you a percentage of your purchase back as cash. Think of it as getting a little reward for every purchase you make. You can use cashback websites or apps that partner with retailers to offer these deals. The key is to use them wisely—only buy what you need, and don't let the allure of cashback tempt you into unnecessary spending. It's about making your regular purchases work for you, allowing you to save while you spend.

Lifestyle changes can also have a big impact on your savings. Take meal prepping, for instance. Instead of eating out or grabbing takeout, spend a bit of time planning and preparing meals at home. Not only is it healthier, but it's also cheaper in the long run. You'll be surprised at how much you can save by cutting down on dining expenses.

Similarly, embracing DIY projects can be a fun and cost-effective alternative to buying new items. Whether it's upcycling old clothes, making gifts, or creating decor, these projects allow you to express creativity while saving money. Minor adjustments like these can lead to significant savings over time.

Mindful spending is another essential element of maximizing your savings. It's about being aware of your spending habits and understanding their impact on your financial goals. Before making a purchase, ask yourself if it aligns with your priorities. Is it something you genuinely need, or is it an impulse buy? By pausing and reflecting, you can make more intentional choices that support your savings efforts. This awareness helps you avoid the pitfalls of mindless spending and keeps your goals focused.

Saving doesn't have to be a chore; it can be fun and rewarding. Consider gamifying the saving process to keep yourself motivated. You could set up saving challenges with friends, like seeing who can save the most in a month or reach a specific goal first. Friendly competition adds an element of excitement and accountability, encouraging everyone to stay on track. You might also implement a reward system for reaching milestones. For instance, treat yourself to something small and meaningful each time you hit a savings target. These incentives make the process enjoyable and give you something to look forward to as you work toward your goals.

Reflection Prompt: Identify Your Saving Hacks

Take a moment to reflect on your current spending habits and think about which saving hacks could work for you. Write down a few changes you'd like to try, whether it's round-up savings, meal prepping, or a new DIY project. Consider setting a specific goal for each hack and track your progress over the next month. This exercise will help you discover new ways to maximize your savings and make the process more engaging.

You can significantly boost your savings by incorporating creative saving techniques, making thoughtful lifestyle changes, and maintaining awareness of your spending. The key is to find what works for you and integrate these strategies into your daily routine. These hacks make saving more manageable and empower you to take control of your financial future. As you continue to explore new ways to save, remember that every small effort counts and contributes to your overall success.

Quiz: The Art of Saving

1. What is the first step to achieving your savings goals?
    a. Spend all your money on something fun.
    b. Start a savings account and set a goal.

    c. Buy the most expensive phone you can find.

    d. Wait until you win the lottery.

2. What's the difference between short-term and long-term goals?

    a. Short-term goals involve saving for smaller things like concert tickets, while long-term goals involve saving for bigger things like college or a car.

    b. Long-term goals are easier to achieve than short-term goals.

    c. Short-term goals take years to achieve, and long-term goals happen quickly.

    d. There's no real difference.

3. What does SMART stand for when setting a savings goal?

    a. Simple, Manageable, Ambitious, Realistic, Timely

    b. Specific, Measurable, Achievable, Relevant, Time-bound

    c. Silly, Money, Apps, Reward, Tools

    d. Save Money and Repeat Tactics

4. If you're saving $50 a month to buy a $600 phone by the end of the year, how long will it take you to reach your goal?

    a. 6 months

    b. 10 months

    c. 12 months

    d. 8 months

5. What's one way to make saving more fun and motivating?

    a. Spend your savings immediately.

    b. Set up a vision board with pictures of what you're saving for.

    c. Only save when you feel like it.

    d. Ignore your progress and check back in a year.

6. True or False: You should only save for things you want right now, not for future goals.
    a. True
    b. False
7. How does compound interest help your savings grow?
    a. By earning interest on your initial deposit and the interest you've already earned.
    b. By magically doubling your money.
    c. By losing interest over time.
    d. By only working for large amounts of money.
8. What's a good way to automate your savings?
    a. Set up automatic transfers from your checking to your savings account.
    b. Always carry cash and put coins in a jar.
    c. Spend as much as possible, then save what's left over.
    d. Ignore your savings until you remember.

Answer Key:

1. b) Start a savings account and set a goal.
2. a) Short-term goals involve saving for smaller things like concert tickets, while long-term goals involve saving for bigger things like college or a car.
3. b) Specific, Measurable, Achievable, Relevant, Time-bound
4. c) 12 months
5. b) Set up a vision board with pictures of what you're saving for.
6. False. You should save for both short-term and long-term goals.
7. a) By earning interest on your initial deposit and the interest you've already earned.

8. a) Set up automatic transfers from your checking to your savings account.

Climbing Savings Summit, we set our sights on distant goals, planting flags for each achievement as we reach new heights.

SECTION 4: UNDERSTANDING CREDIT AND BUILDING A STRONG CREDIT SCORE

"You don't need to raise money. You need to be smart and be focused."

MARK CUBAN

Picture this: you're dreaming about getting your first car or moving into your own apartment. You can almost feel the steering wheel in your hands or visualize your new living space. But here's the catch—those dreams often require more than just saving up your allowance or part-time job earnings, and where credit comes into play. Understanding credit is like having the key to unlock doors to bigger opportunities. It's your financial reputation, and it can influence a whole range of things, from securing loans to renting an apartment. It's not just about borrowing money; it's about showing lenders you're trustworthy and responsible.

So, what exactly is credit? At its core, credit is the ability to borrow money or access goods and services with the agreement to pay later. Think of it as a promise to pay back what you owe, usually with some interest. Having good credit means you've demonstrated reliability in repaying borrowed money, which opens up more financial opportunities. For instance, if you're looking to buy a car, having a solid credit history can make it easier to get a car loan with better terms, like lower interest rates. The same goes for student loans or any other type of borrowing you might need. Your credit also plays a role in renting an apartment, as landlords often check credit scores to see if potential tenants are likely to pay rent consistently.

Credit comes in several forms, each serving different needs. Credit cards are the most well-known type. They allow you to make purchases on borrowed money, which you then pay back monthly. Personal loans are another form, typically used for larger expenses, like medical bills or home renovations. Store cards, offered by many retail outlets, work similarly to credit cards but are often limited to use within the specific store or chain. As a teen, you might not be dealing with all these forms just yet, but understanding them is crucial when you start exploring your options. Each type of credit can impact your credit history differently, influencing your overall financial health.

Having good credit can bring numerous benefits. For starters, it can save you money. When you have a strong credit profile, lenders are more likely to offer you loans with lower interest rates. Having a strong credit profile means you pay fewer extra charges over time, whether for a car, education, or credit cards. Good credit can also lead to better insurance premiums. Insurers often consider credit scores when setting rates, so a higher score could mean paying less for things like car insurance. Essentially, good credit enhances your financial reputation, showing lenders and other institutions that you're a low-risk borrower.

On the flip side, poor credit can make life more challenging. Mismanaging credit, like missing payments or maxing out credit cards, can lead to a lower credit score and can result in difficulty obtaining future credit, as lenders might see you as a risky borrower. Even if you get approved for a loan, you might face higher interest rates, increasing the overall cost of borrowing. It can also affect your ability to rent an apartment or even impact job applications, as some employers review credit history as part of their hiring process. Poor credit can limit your financial opportunities, making it harder to reach your goals.

Understanding credit and its implications is crucial as you step into the world of financial independence. It's about more than just borrowing money—it's about building a positive financial reputation that can open doors to your desired opportunities. Being informed and proactive about your credit can help you make smart decisions, ensuring that you're prepared for the financial responsibilities that come with adulthood.

Reflection Section: How Can Credit Impact Your Future?

Consider your future goals, like buying a car or renting your first apartment. Reflect on how having good credit could help you achieve these dreams. Write down a few ways credit might play a role in your plans and consider steps you can take now to start building a solid credit profile. This exercise encourages you to connect the concept of credit with your personal aspirations, helping you understand its importance on a deeper level.

~

CREDIT CARDS: FRIEND OR FOE?

Credit cards often come with mixed feelings. On the one hand, they're your ticket to building a solid credit history, which can open up financial opportunities down the road. On the other hand, if not used wisely, they can lead to a pile of debt that's tough to climb out of. Let's start with the positives. Credit cards are a great way to start building your credit history. Each time you make a purchase and pay it off on time, you show lenders you're responsible with money. Being responsible can boost your credit score, which is crucial for things like getting a loan or even securing a job. Some credit cards also offer perks like cash-back rewards or travel points, which can be a nice bonus. But remember, these rewards only benefit you if you're not accruing debt to earn them.

Now, let's talk about the risks. The biggest danger with credit cards is the potential to accumulate debt. It's easy to swipe your card for things you want now and worry about paying later. But if you're not careful, those purchases can add up fast, leading to high balances and hefty interest charges, which can quickly spiral into a cycle of debt, where you're paying more in interest than the purchase was worth in the first place. Overspending is a common pitfall. It's tempting to see credit as free money, but it's important to remember that it's borrowed money and comes with strings attached.

So, how can you use credit cards responsibly and avoid these pitfalls? An essential practice is paying off your balance in full each month, which means you're not carrying debt over to the next month and avoiding interest charges. It also helps to understand the terms and conditions of your credit card. Some cards have annual fees or high interest rates, which can catch you off guard if you're unaware. Make it a habit to read the fine print and know exactly what you're agreeing to. This knowledge can save you a lot of money and stress in the long run.

There are also some common misconceptions about credit cards that can lead to trouble. One of the biggest is the belief that making minimum payments is enough. While making at least the minimum payment on time is important to avoid late fees, relying solely on minimum payments can lead to a mountain of debt. This is because interest will continue to accumulate on the remaining balance, making it difficult to pay off over time. Strive to pay more than the minimum whenever possible, ideally paying off each month's total balance. This practice keeps your debt in check and contributes positively to your credit score by showing consistent, responsible use.

Choosing your first credit card can feel overwhelming with so many options available. Look for cards with low interest rates and no annual fees. These features make it more afford-able to carry a balance if you ever need to. Many banks offer student-friendly credit cards designed specifically for young people who are new to credit. These cards often have lower credit limits, which can help you manage spending and reduce the risk of debt. They might also provide educational resources to help you learn about credit management. Don't be swayed by flashy rewards if the card terms aren't favorable. The goal is to find a card that helps you build credit without unnecessary costs.

Credit Card Checklist: What to Look For

- Low-interest rate: This helps keep costs down if you carry a balance.
- No annual fee: Avoid unnecessary charges just for having the card.
- Student-friendly options: Designed for beginners, often with lower limits.
- Simple rewards: If offered, ensure they align with your spending habits.
- Educational resources: Guides and tips for managing credit effectively.

Understanding both the benefits and risks of credit cards is crucial as you start using them. They can be powerful tools for building credit and earning rewards, but only if used wisely. By being informed, setting clear spending limits, and choosing the right card, you can enjoy the advantages of having a credit card without falling into the common traps. Remember, credit cards are not enemies; they're tools that, when used responsibly, can help pave the way to a secure financial future.

$\sim$

THE DOS AND DON'TS OF BUILDING CREDIT AS A TEEN

Building good credit early on is like preparing the soil for a healthy plant to grow. It's all about laying down the right habits that can blossom into solid financial health. One of the most important practices is making timely payments on any bills or loans, such as your phone bill, a small loan, or a subscription service. Paying on time shows lenders that you're reliable and responsible, which can boost your credit history. It's like getting a gold star in school; it's a small action that goes a long way. Another habit to adopt is keeping your credit utilization low, which means not using all your available credit. For example, if your credit limit is $1,000, keep your balance below $300, demonstrate good management, and keep your credit score healthy.

But just as there are good practices, there are also pitfalls to avoid. Frequently applying for new credit accounts is one of them. Each application can result in a hard inquiry, which might lower your credit score slightly. It's like opening too many new accounts on social media; it can become over-whelming and hard to manage. Instead, focus on building a solid history with one or two accounts. Another common mistake is ignoring credit card statements. It might be tempting to just glance at the total amount due, but taking the time to review each charge can help you catch any errors or unauthorized transactions. Plus, it helps you stay aware of your spending habits, allowing you to adjust as needed.

Starting with small, manageable credit lines is a smart way to ease into building credit. You don't need a high limit to make a positive impact. Secured credit cards can be a great starting point. These cards require a cash deposit that serves as your credit limit, minimizing risk. Think of it as training wheels on a bike. It gives you the chance to learn and practice good habits without the temptation of overspending. As you demonstrate responsible use, you might even graduate to a regular credit card, opening up more opportunities.

Monitoring your credit activity is crucial to ensuring every-thing stays on track. Regularly checking your credit report allows you to spot any inaccuracies that could harm your score. It's like checking your social media privacy settings; knowing what's happening with your information is important. Many services offer free annual credit reports, which you can use to review your history and ensure accuracy. This vigilance protects you from not only errors but also potential fraud. If you notice any suspicious activity, you can address it quickly before it causes significant damage.

Interactive Element: Credit Building Checklist

- Pay all bills on time: Set up reminders or automatic payments.
- Maintain low credit utilization: Aim for 30% or less of your credit limit.
- Avoid frequent new credit applications: Only apply when necessary.
- Review statements regularly: Catch errors and understand spending habits.
- Start with secured credit cards: Build credit safely with a deposit-backed limit.
- Monitor your credit report: Use free services to check for inaccuracies and fraud.

By following these guidelines, you can set yourself up for a strong credit profile that will benefit you in many facets of life. Building credit is a marathon, not a sprint. It's about making consistent, positive choices that contribute to a healthy financial future. As you establish these habits, you'll find that managing credit becomes second nature, opening doors to the opportunities you're aiming for.

$\sim$

UNDERSTANDING YOUR CREDIT SCORE: HOW IT'S CALCULATED AND WHY IT MATTERS

Let's break it down: your credit score is like your financial report card, showing how well you handle the money you borrow. This score, typically ranging from 300 to 850, is made up of several different factors, each contributing to your overall financial health. The most significant part is your payment history. It reflects whether you've paid your past credit accounts on time, making up about 35% of your score. Think of it as your track record for keeping promises. If you consistently pay bills late, it can negatively impact your score, much like getting a poor grade for missing assignments.

Next up is credit utilization, which accounts for 30% of your score and is the amount of credit you use compared to your total credit limit. Imagine having a credit card with a $1,000 limit. If you've charged $300, your utilization rate is 30%, which is generally considered good. Keeping it low shows that you're not overly reliant on credit, which lenders like to see. Length of credit history is another factor, making up 15% of your score. The longer your credit accounts have been active, the better. It's like having a long, positive relationship with a teacher who knows your abilities well. Lastly, types of credit, or credit mix, and new credit each account for 10%. Having a mix of credit types, like a credit card and a small personal loan, shows you can handle different kinds of debt responsibly. However, opening several accounts in a short period can signal risk to lenders.

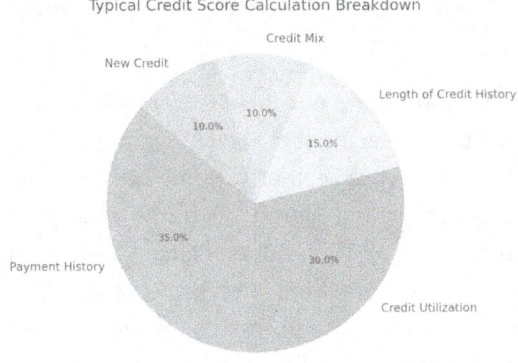

Typical Credit Score Calculation Breakdown

Maintaining a solid credit score opens up a world of financial opportunities. For starters, it makes getting approved for loans and credit much easier. Whether you're applying for a car or a student loan, lenders look at your credit score to decide if you're a safe bet. A high score can also lead to better terms on financial products, which can translate to lower interest rates, saving you money over time. Imagine applying for a loan with a low interest rate because of your excellent credit score—you'd pay back less in interest, leaving more money for other things you want or need. Plus, a good credit score can make it easier to rent an apartment, as landlords often check scores to see if you're likely to pay rent on time.

Improving and maintaining your credit score takes some effort, but it's totally doable with a few smart strategies. Start by making sure you pay all your bills on time. Even if it's just a phone bill, late payments can take a toll on your score. Setting up automatic payments or reminders can help keep you on track. Another tip is to diversify the types of credit you use, but do so responsibly. You don't need to have every type of credit, but having a mix can boost your score. Suppose you've only ever used credit cards. Consider a small personal loan with manageable terms to show you can handle different credit types.

Some fantastic tools are out there to help you keep an eye on your credit score. Credit score tracking apps are a great way to monitor your score regularly. Some even provide tips on how to improve it and alert you to any changes. Many of these apps are free and offer personalized insights, making it easy to see what's working and what needs attention. In addition to apps, you can access your credit report for free once a year from each of the three major credit bureaus. Reviewing your credit report allows you to check for errors or fraudulent activity that could negatively affect your score. Catching these issues early can save you a lot of hassle and help keep your credit in good shape.

Understanding your credit score and how it's calculated is crucial for making informed financial decisions. It's not just a number; it's a snapshot of your financial habits and reliability. By focusing on the key factors that influence your score and using the right tools to monitor your progress, you can build and maintain a credit score that opens doors to exciting opportunities. Whether you're dreaming of buying your first car, pursuing higher education, or securing a place of your own, a strong credit score can help make those dreams a reality.

$\sim$

AVOIDING CREDIT PITFALLS: STAYING OUT OF DEBT

Navigating the credit maze can be a real headache. Here's the lowdown: one of the sneakiest ways people get tripped up is by whipping out the credit card for all the small stuff. You know, grabbing a latte or snagging a cool tee. It seems no biggie at first, but, whoa, do those charges stack up quickly! Suddenly, you're eyeballing a credit card statement that's way heftier than you bargained for. Getting too cozy with credit for your day-to-day buys is like digging yourself into a financial pit that just gets deeper and deeper. It's key to catch yourself if you're defaulting to credit a tad too often and finding yourself reaching for that plastic for the usual expenses. It might be time to pivot to cash or a debit card for your daily dough. Making the switch can be a game-changer in sticking to your budget and steering clear of the debt dungeon.

Let's chat about another pitfall lurking around: the allure of the minimum payment. When you're pinching pennies, it's super tempting just to pay the smallest amount due. But here's the catch – it stretches out your debt and cranks up the interest you're forking over in the long run. Think of your credit card debt as a video game villain. The more you ignore it, the stronger it gets. Making only the minimum payment? That's like hitting the boss with the weakest weapon, barely making a dent. Your goal? Equip yourself with the best gear to defeat it swiftly—paying off more each month. Aim to clear as much of your balance as you can each month. This tactic slashes the total interest you'll end up paying and frees you from debt's grip sooner. Struggling to pay more than the minimum? Time for a budget deep-dive to spot where you can trim the fat and reallocate some funds toward squashing that credit card debt.

Are you already caught in the debt web? Don't hit the panic button. There's a solid game plan for digging your way out. Kick-off by targeting the debts with the nastiest interest rates first. Tackling the debt with the highest interest rates first is akin to facing off against the ultimate boss in a game —a challenging endeavor but incredibly satisfying when conquered. Once those high-interest headaches are history, you can shift your focus to the rest of your debt. Sketching out a debt repayment strategy is a smart move. Jot down all your debts, their interest rates, and minimum payments, then map out your attack. This strategy is like having a personal finance GPS – it keeps you on track and pumped to reach your debt-free destination.

Staying disciplined with your finances is your secret weapon in the credit battle. Set spending caps for yourself and stick to them like glue. Getting swept up in the thrill of snagging what you want is a breeze, but reigning in those impulses is crucial for keeping your finances fit. Tempted by a purchase? Pause and ask yourself if it's really budget-friendly and necessary. This gut check can curb impulse buys and keep your credit use in healthy territory. Another pro tip: leverage a budgeting app to monitor your spending. Seeing where your cash is going can be a huge motivator to keep your spending in line.

Are you feeling swamped by debt? It's totally okay to reach out for help. A financial counselor can be your ally, offering strategies to manage your debt and crafting a payment plan you can actually stick to. They're also pros at dishing out budgeting and financial planning wisdom to dodge future debt disasters. Touching base with a credit counselor isn't waving the white flag – it's a savvy move toward getting back in the financial driver's seat. Many offer their expertise for free or at a low cost, so getting help won't break the bank. They're there to help you negotiate with creditors, consolidate your debts, and support you on your journey to financial steadiness.

Credit & Strong Credit Score Quiz

1. Why is having good credit important?
   a. It allows you to avoid paying rent
   b. It can help you get loans with better interest rates and rent an apartment
   c. It makes you eligible for free products
   d. It's not important at all
2. Which of the following is NOT a way to build good credit?
   a. Paying bills on time
   b. Maxing out your credit card regularly
   c. Keeping your credit utilization low
   d. Checking your credit report for errors
3. What percentage of your credit score is based on your payment history?
   a. 50%
   b. 35%
   c. 25%
   d. 15%
4. What is one risk of making only the minimum payment on your credit card each month?
   a. You'll be charged late fees
   b. Your credit score will increase
   c. You'll accumulate more debt due to interest charges
   d. You'll get reward points faster
5. What's the ideal credit utilization rate to maintain a healthy credit score?
   a. 100%
   b. 50%
   c. 30% or less
   d. 75%
6. Which of the following is a benefit of using a credit card responsibly?
   a. You can avoid paying for purchases altogether

b. You can build a strong credit history
c. You can spend unlimited amounts without consequence
d. You don't need to make any payments

Answer Key

1. b) It can help you get loans with better interest rates and rent an apartment
2. b) Maxing out your credit card regularly
3. b) 35%
4. c) You'll accumulate more debt due to interest charges
5. c) 30% or less
6. b) You can build a strong credit history

As we wrap up this Section, remember that avoiding credit pitfalls is all about being mindful and proactive. By understanding common traps and implementing strategies to manage and pay down debt, you're setting yourself up for a solid financial future. Financial discipline and seeking help when needed are crucial components of this journey. Next, we'll explore how investing can become a powerful tool in your financial toolkit, opening new avenues for growth and security.

At Credit Castle, we build our defenses, learning to construct a strong credit score that protects us from financial setbacks.

SECTION 5: INTRODUCTION TO INVESTING

"Money doesn't grow on trees, but it can grow if you know how to invest it."

KANYE WEST

Imagine you're at a fair, and there's a game that promises a prize if you play smart. The game is all about investing, and the prize? Building wealth and securing your financial future. Now, you might be thinking, "Investing sounds like something only adults need to worry about." But here's the secret: the earlier you start, the better your chances of winning that prize. Investing isn't just for grown-ups with suits and briefcases; it's for anyone who wants to grow their money, including you. Whether saving for college, a car, or just building a financial cushion, investing can be your ticket to achieving those goals.

Let's break it down. At its core, investing is about putting your money to work to earn more over time. One of the most common ways to invest is through stocks. Imagine stocks as tiny pieces of a company. When you buy a stock, you own a small part of that company. If the company does well, your stock's value goes up, and you can sell it for more than you paid. It's like buying a concert ticket for a popular band and selling it when the demand (and price) skyrockets. But remember, stocks can be risky. Their value can go up or down, so preparing for both is essential.

Bonds are another investment option, and they work quite differently. When you buy a bond, you're essentially lending money to a corporation or government, and in return, they pay you interest over time. It's like lending your friend money to buy a game, and they pay you back with a little extra for your help. Bonds are generally considered safer than stocks, but they offer lower returns. They're like the steady, reliable friend who's always there to pay you back on time.

Then there are mutual funds, which combine (or pool) money from many investors to purchase a diversified mix of stocks, bonds, or other securities. Think of it as joining forces with other players to get a better shot at winning the game. Professional managers decide where to invest the pooled money, aiming to make it grow. This means you get the benefit of their expertise without having to make all the tough decisions yourself. Mutual funds are a great way to diversify or spread out your investments, which helps reduce risk.

Diversification is a key part of investing. It's like not putting all your eggs in one basket. By spreading your money across different types of investments, like stocks and bonds, you're less likely to lose everything if one investment doesn't do well. It's about finding a balance that works for you. For example, you might invest part of your money in stocks for potential high returns and another part in bonds for stability. This way, if the stock market dips, your bonds can help cushion the blow.

Index funds and Exchange-Traded Funds (ETFs) are excellent starting points for beginners. Index funds track a specific market index, like the S&P 500, and offer a low-cost way to invest in a broad range of stocks. It's like buying a little bit of each company in the index, spreading out your investment. ETFs are similar but trade like stocks on an exchange, providing flexibility and diversification. They're great for young investors who want to dip their toes into the investing world without diving in headfirst.

Before you jump into investing, take time to research potential investments. Use financial news sources to keep up with company updates and market trends. Understanding a company's performance history can help you make informed decisions. It's like checking reviews before buying a new gadget; you want to know what you're getting into. Analyzing historical performance data can also give you insights into how an investment might behave in the future.

Interactive Element: Start Your Investment Research

Grab a notebook and choose one company or
fund that interests you. Use financial news
websites to gather information. Note down
the company's recent performance, any
major news, and your thoughts on its future.
This exercise will help you get comfortable

with researching investments and making
informed choices.

Investing might sound complex, but it's all
about understanding the basics and making
decisions that align with your goals. By
learning about stocks, bonds, mutual funds,
and the importance of diversification,
you're setting yourself up for success.
Whether you're saving for something
specific or just looking to grow your money,
investing can be a powerful tool in your
financial toolkit. You've got the potential to
become a savvy investor, and this Section is
just the beginning.

~

THE POWER OF EARLY INVESTING: STARTING YOUNG

Let's talk about why getting into investing early is like
planting a tree. The sooner you plant it, the more time it has
to grow and bear fruit. Investing works in a similar way
through something called compounding returns.
Compounding returns are where you earn returns not just
on your initial investment but also on the accumulated gains
over time. Imagine planting a sapling that grows taller and
stronger each year. With investing, the earlier you start, the
more time your money has to grow exponentially. You have
the advantage of watching your small initial investments
snowball into substantial sums over decades.

Consider this: if you start investing at 15 instead of waiting
until 25, you have an extra ten years for your money to grow.
It's like getting a head start in a race. A small amount

invested when you're young can grow into something much larger than if you wait until later. For instance, investing just $100 a month starting at 15 can yield significantly more by the time you reach retirement age compared to starting the same investment at 25. That's the magic of compounding in action. Over time, those early investments tend to outperform those made later because they've had more time to benefit from compounding. The earlier you start, the more your money can work for you, even with modest contributions.

Building the habit of investing on a regular basis is crucial. It's like flexing a muscle; the more you do it, the stronger it gets. Starting with small, manageable amounts makes it easier to stick with it. You don't need a lot of money to begin investing. Even small contributions can add up over time. Setting up automatic contributions to your investment account can help make this process seamless. It's like setting a schedule for watering your plants; consistency is key. By automating your investments, you ensure that a portion of your money goes towards your future without you having to think about it. This habit not only builds your investments but also instills financial discipline.

The long-term security provided by early investing cannot be overstated. It's about setting yourself up for financial freedom and independence. Imagine reaching adulthood with a solid retirement fund already in place. That's the power of starting young. It gives you more flexibility in your investment strategies. You can afford to take more risks with your investments because you have time to recover from any downturns. It's like having a safety net that allows you to explore different opportunities without worrying about immediate consequences. As you watch your investments grow, you gain a sense of financial stability and confidence that can set you apart from your peers.

Consider your future goals, like buying a house, traveling the world, or even retiring comfortably. Starting to invest early provides the foundation for achieving these dreams. It's about more than just accumulating wealth; it's about creating options and opportunities for yourself. The financial independence that comes from early investing is empowering. It allows you to make choices that align with your values and aspirations without being constrained by financial limitations. This is your chance to take control of your financial destiny and build a future that reflects your ambitions.

Early investing is not just about the money you put in; it's about the time you give your money to grow. By starting young, you're leveraging one of the most powerful forces in finance—time. It's your ally, working tirelessly to grow your investments while you focus on living your life. Making small, regular investments is like setting the stage for your financial future. Over time, these efforts compound, creating a ripple effect that can lead to significant financial security and independence. So, why not start now and give your future self the gift of financial freedom?

～

RISK AND REWARD: UNDERSTANDING INVESTMENT BASICS

Imagine standing at the edge of a diving board. The water below is inviting, but there's always that moment of hesitation. Investing is a bit like that. The potential reward is enticing, yet there's a risk involved. In the world of investing, risk and reward go hand in hand. Higher risks often come with the chance for higher returns. Think of the stock market, where prices can go up and down like a roller coaster. This volatility means you could gain a lot, but there's also the chance of losing money. On the flip side, bonds tend to be more stable, offering lower returns but with less risk. It's like choosing between a thrilling roller coaster and a gentle Ferris wheel. Each has its own appeal, depending on how adventurous you're feeling.

Understanding your comfort level with risk is crucial in investing and is known as your risk tolerance—the amount of risk you're willing to take on for potential rewards. Some people naturally enjoy the thrill and are comfortable with the ups and downs of the stock market. Others prefer keeping things steady and secure, opting for investments like bonds. To figure out where you stand, consider taking a risk assessment quiz. These quizzes use scenarios to help you identify your comfort zone, guiding you toward investments that match your personality. It's like taking a personality test for your money, helping you make choices that feel right to you.

Managing investment risk is all about finding balance. One strategy is diversification. Diversification means spreading your investments across different asset classes, like mixing stocks, bonds, and maybe even some real estate. It's similar to not putting all your eggs in one basket. If one investment performs poorly, others might balance it out. Investing in low-risk government bonds can help keep things steady, balancing out riskier investments. It's like having a safety net that helps you handle the ups and downs, keeping your overall plan more stable.

When evaluating investments, it's helpful to understand risk-adjusted returns. This concept looks at the amount of return earned relative to the risk taken. Imagine you're comparing two different rides at an amusement park. One is a wild roller coaster with many twists and turns, while the other is a smooth, predictable ride. Both might offer similar excitement, but the roller coaster involves more risk. The Sharpe ratio is a tool used to measure this balance in investments. It helps you see how much return you're getting for your risk, guiding you in making smarter investment choices. This ratio is especially useful when comparing similar investments, allowing you to choose the one that offers the best balance of risk and reward.

As you explore investing, remember that risk isn't something to fear but to understand. It's about assessing your comfort level, diversifying wisely, and seeking the right balance between risk and reward. By taking calculated risks, you give yourself the opportunity to grow your investments over time. Keep in mind that everyone's risk tolerance is different, and what works for someone else might not be right for you. Finding an approach that aligns with your goals and comfort level is key. With the right mindset and strategies, you can confidently navigate the world of investing, making choices that support your financial aspirations.

Sample Quiz: Investment Risk & Style*

1. How do you feel about investing in something that could potentially lose money in the short term but could grow over time?
   a. I want to avoid losses at all costs.
   b. I'm okay with a bit of risk for potential growth.
   c. I'm comfortable with taking bigger risks for the chance of higher returns.
2. Imagine you've invested $100, and the value drops to $85 in a month. What's your next move?
   a. Sell right away—I don't want to lose more.
   b. Hold on and wait for it to recover.

   c. Buy more while the price is lower, expecting it to
      bounce back.
3. When making an investment, how long are you
   willing to leave your money invested?
   a. Less than 1 year.
   b. 1–3 years.
   c. 5+ years.

Quiz Analysis:

If you answered mostly A's, you have a low-risk tolerance.

If you answered mostly B's, you have a moderate risk
tolerance.

If you answered mostly C's, you have a high-risk tolerance.

~

FINDING YOUR INVESTMENT STYLE: WHAT TYPE OF INVESTOR ARE YOU?

Imagine discovering a way of investing that fits you, like
your favorite pair of sneakers. Investing isn't a one-size-fits-
all deal. Different styles suit different goals and personalities.
Let's break down some popular investment styles to help you
find your fit. Growth investing is like being on the lookout
for the next big thing. You're investing in companies
expected to grow at an above-average rate compared to
others. It's about spotting potential early and riding the wave
of expansion. Think of tech startups or innovative companies changing the game.

On the other hand, value investing is like bargain hunting.
You're seeking stocks that are undervalued by the market,
hoping they'll eventually rise to their true worth. It's about

patience and believing in the intrinsic value of a company. Then, there's the choice between active and passive investing. Active investing involves hands-on management, frequently buying and selling based on market conditions. It's like being a coach, strategizing every move. Passive investing is more relaxed. It involves buying and holding investments for the long haul, aiming to mirror the performance of a market index. It's like setting your playlist on shuffle and enjoying the ride without constant adjustments.

Finding your investment style begins with understanding your own personality traits. Are you someone who enjoys taking risks and thrives on excitement? Or do you prefer stability and predictability? Your answers can guide you toward a style that resonates with you. Personality trait analysis can be a handy tool here. It's like a personality quiz but for your financial habits. Consider what excites you—do you love diving into details, analyzing data, and making quick decisions? You might lean toward active investing. Or do you prefer sitting back and letting things unfold over time? Passive investing might be more your speed. Reflect on what aligns with your values and comfort level. This self-awareness helps ensure your investment choices feel natural and sustainable.

Your personal goals play a huge role in shaping your investment strategy. It's important to align your investment style with your goal. Are you saving for a short-term goal, like a new laptop or a trip next summer? Or are you focused on long-term aspirations, like college tuition or a down payment on a house? Short-term goals might benefit from a more conservative, stable approach, ensuring funds aren't tied up when you need them. Long-term goals allow you to take on more risk, potentially reaping higher rewards over time. Your investment choices should reflect these timelines, aligning with when you'll need the money and how comfortable you are with potential fluctuations.

Experimentation is key to discovering what works best for you. Just like trying on different styles of clothes, testing various investment strategies can help you find your perfect fit. Don't be afraid to explore different approaches to see which resonates with you. Simulated trading platforms can be a great way to practice without any risk. These platforms let you try out investment strategies in a virtual environment, giving you a taste of how different styles play out in real time. It's like a dress rehearsal before the big show. You can gain confidence and insight into how different strategies work while honing your investing skills. This hands-on experience is invaluable, allowing you to learn from mistakes and successes without any financial consequences.

Investing is a personal journey, and finding your style is all about aligning your strategy with your personality and goals. By understanding different approaches, analyzing your traits, and experimenting with various styles, you can develop an investment plan that feels right for you. Whether you're a growth seeker, a value hunter, or somewhere in between, there's an investment style that matches your rhythm. The key is to stay curious, keep learning, and remember that your investment style can evolve as you do.

Sample Quiz: Finding Your Investment Style*

1. Do you prefer actively managing your investments by frequently buying and selling?
   a. No, I prefer to invest and leave it alone.
   b. Sometimes, depending on the situation.
   c. Yes, I like being involved and making frequent decisions.

Response Breakdown:

a. Passive investing style.
b. Moderate/Hybrid investing style.
c. Active investing style.

2. How do you feel about investing in fast-growing companies, even risky ones?
   o I'm not interested in risky companies, even if they're growing.
   o I'll take a chance on some, but not all.
   o I'm excited about the potential of fast-growing companies, even risky ones.

Response Breakdown:

a. Value investor.
b. Balanced investor.
c. Growth investor.

3. Are you more focused on finding undervalued investments or companies with high growth potential?
   a. I prefer finding undervalued companies that will rise to their true worth.
   b. I'm open to both undervalued companies and growth potential.
   c. I'm mainly looking for companies with high growth potential, even if they are expensive.

Response Breakdown:

a. a) Value investor.
b. b) Balanced investor.

c. c) Growth investor.

*Note:

These quizzes are just samples to give you a basic idea of your risk tolerance and investment style. They're meant to help you start thinking about how you approach investing, but remember, investing is personal and can be complex. For a more in-depth understanding, check out comprehensive quizzes online or talk to a financial advisor (either in person or virtually) who can guide you based on your specific situation. Getting expert advice is key when it comes to making smart money moves!

∽

USING INVESTMENT APPS: HOW TECHNOLOGY CAN HELP YOU INVEST

Imagine having a tool in your pocket that makes investing as easy as scrolling through social media. That's what investment apps do. They're designed to make investing accessible and user-friendly, especially for beginners. Apps like Robinhood and Acorns have changed the game, allowing you to start investing with just a few taps on your smartphone. Robinhood, for instance, lets you trade stocks and ETFs without paying commissions, making it a popular choice for those just starting out. It's like having a front-row seat to the stock market, where you can watch your investments grow in real time. Then there's Acorns, which takes a different approach by rounding up your everyday purchases and investing the spare change. It's a simple way to start building a portfolio without needing a large sum of money upfront.

These apps aren't just about buying and selling; they offer a wealth of resources to help you learn and manage your investments. Many come with educational tools and tutorials, providing insights into market trends and investment strategies. Think of it as having a virtual mentor guiding you through your investing journey. With real-time portfolio management, you can easily track your investments, set goals, and adjust your strategy based on market conditions. It's like having a dashboard showing exactly how your money works for you. This transparency helps demystify investing, making it feel less intimidating and more approachable.

Choosing the right investment app can be like shopping for the perfect pair of shoes. You want something that fits comfortably and meets your needs. Start by considering the fees and commissions associated with each app. While many offer commission-free trades, some might charge for certain features or services. It's important to read the fine print so there are no surprises later. User experience is another crucial factor. Look for apps with intuitive interfaces that make navigation easy. You don't want to spend all your time figuring out how to use the app instead of investing. Customer support is also key. An app with responsive support can make a big difference if you run into questions or issues.

Once you've chosen an app, take advantage of its features to enhance your investing experience. Many apps include stock analysis tools, providing detailed information about different investments. These tools help you make informed decisions by offering insights into company performance, financial health, and market trends. Goal-setting and progress-tracking features are also valuable. They allow you to set specific investment targets and monitor your progress, keeping you motivated and on track. It's like having a personal coach cheering you on as you work towards your financial goals.

Visual Element: Investment App Checklist

- ☑ **No or low fees:** Ensure the app offers commission-free trades or low fees.
- ☑ **User-friendly interface**: Choose apps that are easy to navigate.
- ☑ **Educational resources**: Look for tutorials and insights within the app.
- ☑ **Responsive customer support**: Ensure you have help when needed.
- ☑ **Stock analysis tools**: Use features that provide investment insights.
- ☑ **Goal-setting**: Utilize features to track your investment targets.

Incorporating technology into your investing strategy can make a world of difference. It simplifies the process, breaking down barriers that might have kept you from investing before. With the right app, you gain not only a platform for trading but also a comprehensive resource for learning and growing as an investor. As you explore these tools, you'll find that investing becomes less about numbers and more about pursuing your financial dreams. With these digital allies at your fingertips, you're well-equipped to make informed decisions and set yourself up for success.

Activity: Build Your Investment Portfolio!**

Imagine you have $1,000 to invest. Using what you've learned about different types of investments like stocks, bonds, mutual funds, and ETFs, decide how you want to allocate your money. Will you take more risks for potentially higher returns or play it safe with steady investments? Use the following table to create your portfolio, then reflect on your choices.

Investment Portfolio Table:

Stocks:	$_____	High risk, high reward
Bonds:	$_____	Lower risk, steady returns
Mutual Funds/ETFs:	$_____	Diversified, balanced risk
Cash Savings:	$_____	No risk, just in case

After building your portfolio, consider these questions:

1. Why did you choose to invest more in one area than another?
2. How do you feel about taking risks with your money?
3. What would you do if your stocks lost value?
4. How does your portfolio balance risk and reward?

This activity helps you consider how different investment options align with your risk tolerance and financial goals. Balancing risk and reward is a key part of successful investing.

Note:

This portfolio-building exercise is a sample designed to get you thinking about how you might invest money. However, investing can be complex, and consulting with a financial advisor or using comprehensive tools (online or in person) is important to guide your real-life investment decisions. Understanding your risk tolerance and investment goals fully is crucial to making smart financial choices!

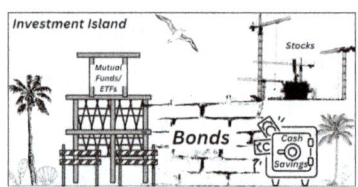

On Investment Island, you're the Architect, using stocks as cranes, bonds as foundation brick wall, mutual funds as scaffolding, and cash savings as secure vaults to build a strong financial future.

SECTION 6: MAKING MONEY WORK FOR YOU

"I never thought I'd make this much money, so a number is not going to stop me from working."

RIHANNA

E ver thought about how cool it would be to earn money without clocking into a traditional job? Imagine turning your love for dogs into a cash-making venture or making art in your spare time and selling it online. Welcome to the world of side hustles—flexible gigs that let you earn on your own terms. Side hustles are all about autonomy and flexibility, offering a chance to make money while doing something you genuinely enjoy. They don't require the rigid schedules of traditional jobs, meaning you can fit them around school, hobbies, and social life. You get to decide when, where, and how you work, allowing you to balance your time as you see fit.

Think about offering dog walking or pet sitting services in your neighborhood. If you love animals, this can be both rewarding and profitable. People often need someone trustworthy to care for their pets, especially during busy workweeks or vacations. By offering these services, you not only get to spend time with adorable pets but also earn money doing it. Another popular option is babysitting for family and friends. Babysitting can be a great way to earn if you're good with kids. It's a responsible job that can teach you patience and creativity while providing a steady income. Plus, it's usually done during evenings or weekends, fitting well into a teen's schedule.

Your hobbies and skills can also be turned into income-generating activities. Are you into crafting or painting? Platforms like Etsy allow you to sell homemade crafts or art, reaching customers far beyond your local area. This brings in money and lets you improve your skills and gain business experience. If you play an instrument, consider offering music lessons to younger kids. Parents are always on the lookout for tutors, and teaching music can be a fun way to share your passion while earning. It's about finding what you love and figuring out how to make it pay. The key is to leverage your unique talents and interests, turning them into something others value and are willing to pay for.

Side hustles come with their own set of benefits and challenges. On the plus side, they offer flexible hours, meaning you can work when it suits you. This flexibility is perfect for managing other commitments, ensuring you don't miss out on important schoolwork or social events. Side hustles also allow you to develop valuable skills, from customer service to time management, which can be useful in future careers. However, they also require careful time management, as it's easy to let work spill over into your personal life. Inconsistent income can be another challenge, as side hustles might not always provide a steady paycheck. Budgeting wisely and having a financial safety net to fall back on during slow periods is important.

Marketing and promoting your side hustle effectively is crucial for success. Social media can be a powerful tool for reaching potential clients. Platforms like Instagram and Facebook allow you to showcase your skills and services, reaching a wide audience with minimal cost. Share photos of your work, post testimonials, and engage with followers to build a loyal customer base. Networking within local community groups is another effective strategy. Attend local events or join online forums where your target audience hangs out. Word of mouth is powerful; making connections can lead to new opportunities. The more people know about your hustle, the more likely you are to succeed.

Interactive Element: Create Your Side Hustle Plan

Take a moment to brainstorm your side hustle. What hobbies or skills could you turn into an income stream? Write down a list of ideas and pick one that excites you the most. Next, outline a simple plan—who your target audience is, how you will reach them, and what tools you will use to promote your hustle. Consider setting up a social media page or joining local groups to spread the word. This exercise will help you visualize your side hustle and take actionable steps toward making it a reality.

Side hustles are a fantastic way to explore your passions while earning money. They offer a unique blend of freedom, responsibility, and creativity, allowing you to learn and grow in ways traditional jobs might not. The possibilities are endless, whether it's walking dogs, selling art, or teaching music. Embrace the opportunity to make money on your terms, and who knows—you might even discover a career path you hadn't considered before.

∼

FREELANCING 101: TURNING SKILLS INTO INCOME

Imagine having the freedom to work whenever you want, choosing projects that interest you, and getting paid for your unique talents. That's what freelancing is all about. It's a fantastic way for teens to earn money by using skills they already have. Whether you're into graphic design or writing, freelancing can be a perfect fit. Picture this: a local coffee shop needs a new logo, and they turn to you because of your knack for creating eye-catching designs. Or maybe a website needs fresh content and chooses you to write engaging articles. These are just a couple of examples of how you can turn your skills into income on a project-by-project basis. Freelancing allows you to explore your passions while gaining valuable work experience and earning money on your terms.

Now, you might wonder where to find these freelancing gigs. That's where platforms like Fiverr and Upwork come into play. These websites connect freelancers with clients looking for services, making them ideal for beginners. On Fiverr, you can offer services starting at five dollars, setting your own rates, and building your profile as you gain experience. On the other hand, Upwork provides a diverse network of clients and projects with tools to help you manage time and payments. These platforms are user-friendly and provide a great starting point for teens looking to dive into freelancing. They offer opportunities in a wide range of fields, ensuring you can find projects that match your interests and skills.

To succeed in freelancing, building a strong portfolio is crucial. Think of your portfolio as your personal showcase— it's what potential clients will look at to assess your capabilities. Start by creating an online portfolio website where you can display your work. Include samples of previous projects, even if they're just personal or school assignments that demonstrate your skills. Additionally, gather testimonials from satisfied clients or teachers who can vouch for your work ethic and creativity. This feedback adds credibility and helps potential clients trust in your abilities. A well-organized and visually appealing portfolio can significantly boost your chances of landing freelance gigs. It's your digital résumé highlighting your strengths and giving clients a glimpse of what you can offer.

Managing freelance projects can be a juggling act, especially when you're handling multiple tasks at once. Organization is key. Consider using project management tools like Trello, which allows you to create boards for each project, set deadlines, and track progress. These tools help you stay on top of your workload, ensuring you meet deadlines without feeling overwhelmed. Communication is another critical aspect. Set clear expectations with your clients from the start. Discuss deadlines, project details, and any revisions upfront to avoid misunderstandings later. Keeping an open line of communication helps build trust and ensures everyone is on the same page throughout the project. It's about creating a professional relationship where both parties feel comfortable and informed.

Freelancing as a teen offers a glimpse into the professional world, with the flexibility to learn and grow at your own pace. It allows you to hone your skills, build a network, and earn money doing what you love. Whether it's designing graphics for a new business or writing articles for a blog, each project is an opportunity to develop your talents and gain experience that will serve you well in the future. The freedom to choose your projects and work schedule makes freelancing an appealing option for those looking to balance work with other commitments. It's about finding the right fit for your interests and skill set and creating a path that aligns with your personal and professional goals.

$\sim$

ENTREPRENEURSHIP: STARTING YOUR OWN TEEN BUSINESS

Imagine turning an idea into something real, something that's yours. That's the magic of entrepreneurship. It's about taking your passions and creating a business that reflects who you are. Whether you're passionate about fashion and want to start a custom T-shirt line, or you love cars and see a market for a local car wash, entrepreneurship offers a canvas for your creativity. The possibilities are endless, and the best part is you're the one calling the shots. This isn't just about making money; it's about doing what you love and learning along the way. Each step you take is a chance to grow and learn something new.

Launching a small business starts with a solid plan. Your business plan is your roadmap. Begin by outlining your services or products and setting clear goals. Consider what makes your business unique and how you'll stand out. Next, consider the practicalities—do you need any permits or licenses to operate? For example, a lawn care business might require specific equipment or permits to work in certain areas. Researching these details early on is crucial to avoid any legal hiccups. This stage is about laying a solid foundation, ensuring you have everything in place to get started smoothly.

Understanding your market is vital. Having a great idea is not enough; you need to know who will buy your product or service and why. Conducting market research helps you gather insights into what your potential customers want. You could start by conducting surveys or informal interviews with people in your community. This feedback is invaluable —it helps you refine your offerings and tailor your business to meet customer needs. Listening to your customers' opinions can guide you in making improvements or adjustments, ensuring your business stays relevant and appealing. It's about building a relationship with your market, understanding their preferences, and aligning your services with their expectations.

Managing your business finances is a big piece of the puzzle. Budgeting is crucial. You'll need to set competitive prices that cover your costs while staying attractive to customers. Think about everything from material expenses to your time. Tracking expenses and revenue is essential; accounting software can simplify this process. These tools help you keep an eye on your financial health, making it easier to see where you're making money and where you might be spending too much. This insight is vital for making informed decisions and ensuring your business remains profitable. Managing finances effectively means you can reinvest in your business, expand your offerings, or even save for future projects.

Visual Element: Business Plan Template

> Creating a business plan might sound daunting, but it doesn't have to be. Use a simple business plan template to outline your ideas. Break it down into sections: your business name, the services or products you offer, your target market, marketing strategies, and financial projections. This template will help you organize your thoughts and focus on the essentials, providing a clear path from idea to execution.

Running a business also involves day-to-day management, which includes everything from customer service to operations. You'll need to juggle various tasks, from responding to customer inquiries to managing inventory if you're selling products. It's about staying organized and maintaining a smooth workflow. Time management is your ally here. Setting a schedule or using tools to plan your day can help you stay on top of your responsibilities, ensuring nothing falls through the cracks. It's about finding a rhythm that works for you and helps you keep your business running efficiently.

Entrepreneurship as a teen is more than just a way to make money. It's a journey of discovery, a chance to explore what you're passionate about and see it come to life. It teaches you skills that go beyond the classroom, from problem-solving to communication. Each challenge you face is an opportunity to learn and grow, building resilience and adaptability. Whether launching a new product line or expanding your customer base, every step is a milestone on your entrepreneurial path.

MONEY MANAGEMENT FOR EARNERS: HANDLING INCOME WISELY

Whether through a part-time job or a hobby-turned-business, earning money feels pretty awesome. But managing that income wisely is where the real magic happens. Think of it like playing a strategic game, where budgeting and financial planning are your best moves. Setting aside a portion of your income for savings is crucial. It's like planting seeds for future growth. Whether you're saving for a new gadget, a trip, or even college, having a savings plan ensures that your hard-earned money is working for you. Tracking all sources of income from various jobs is equally important. Sometimes, it's easy to lose track of where your money comes from, especially if juggling multiple gigs. Keeping tabs on every dollar helps you see the bigger picture and make informed decisions about spending and saving.

Digital tools can make managing your income a breeze, simplifying the process and saving you time. Budgeting apps like Mint offer a convenient way to track your financial activities. With features that categorize spending and provide insights into your habits, these apps act as personal financial advisors in your pocket. They remind you of upcoming bills, help you set budgets, and even alert you when your spending limits are nearing. It's about using technology to simplify your money management, making it less of a chore and more of a routine. These tools also help identify areas where you might be overspending, allowing you to adjust your habits and maximize your savings.

Prioritizing your financial goals is key to effective money management. It's like setting a GPS for your finances, guiding you toward what matters most. Start by identifying your short-term and long-term goals. Short-term goals might include saving for a concert or a new outfit, while long-term goals could be buying a car or funding your education. Once you know what you're aiming for, allocate your income accordingly. Decide how much you'll save for each goal and stick to it. It keeps you focused but also prevents you from spending impulsively. It's about aligning your spending with your priorities, ensuring your money is directed towards things that truly matter to you.

Building an emergency fund is another cornerstone of smart income management. Life is unpredictable, and having a financial cushion can save you from unexpected expenses. Regular contributions to a separate savings account can build this fund over time. It doesn't have to be a massive amount—a small, consistent addition from each paycheck can grow into a substantial safety net. This fund is your go-to for emergencies, whether a medical bill or a sudden car repair. It provides peace of mind, knowing you're prepared for whatever comes your way. It's about being proactive, not reactive when it comes to your finances.

Handling income wisely involves more than just saving and budgeting. It's about understanding your relationship with money and making conscious choices. Reflect on your spending habits and consider what drives them. Are you spending to keep up with friends, or are you investing in experiences that enrich your life? Being mindful of these choices helps you spend intentionally, ensuring every dollar aligns with your values. It's not about depriving yourself but about making sure your spending supports your goals and aspirations.

Consider setting up automatic transfers to your savings and emergency fund accounts. This way, you're consistently saving without even thinking about it. Automation can be a game-changer, reducing the temptation to spend money elsewhere. It's a simple yet effective strategy to ensure you consistently contribute to your financial goals. Plus, it helps you build a habit of saving, turning it into a natural part of your financial routine. This kind of discipline is what sets successful money managers apart.

Making the most of your income requires a thoughtful approach. It's about balancing enjoyment with responsibility, ensuring you're living in the moment, and planning for the future. With the right mindset and tools, you can handle your income wisely and set yourself up for financial success both now and in the years to come.

BALANCING WORK AND LIFE: MANAGING TIME EFFECTIVELY

Finding the perfect balance between earning money and enjoying life can feel like walking a tightrope. Creating a daily schedule that allows time for work, study, and leisure is crucial. Imagine your day as a blank slate, and you're the artist deciding what colors to splash where. Start by mapping out your priorities. Allocate specific hours for schoolwork, ensuring you're not scrambling to finish assignments at the last minute. Then, slot in your work hours or time for your side hustle. Don't forget to include breaks and downtime, too. These moments are essential for recharging and maintaining your energy. It's about creating a rhythm that flows and feels natural, allowing you to accomplish tasks without feeling overwhelmed.

Taking on too much can quickly lead to burnout, affecting your mental and physical health. It might seem tempting to say "yes" to every opportunity that comes your way, thinking it's the best way to maximize your potential. But overcommitting is like trying to juggle too many balls at once; eventually, something will drop. Recognizing signs of stress and burnout early can save you from crashing. Are you feeling constantly tired, irritable, or unable to focus? These might be signals that you're stretching yourself too thin. It's important to listen to your body and mind, understanding when it's time to step back and breathe. Remember, taking care of yourself is as important as meeting deadlines or making money.

Setting boundaries is a key strategy for maintaining a balanced lifestyle. Clearly define your work commitments and communicate your availability to clients or employers. Let them know your non-work hours and stand firm in keeping those boundaries. This clarity not only helps you protect your personal time but also sets expectations for others. It's about creating a space where you can focus on work when it's time and fully relax when it's not. Setting these limits helps prevent work from encroaching on your personal life, ensuring you have time for family, friends, and hobbies. It's about finding that sweet spot where work and life complement each other rather than compete.

Maximizing productivity during work hours allows you to do more in less time, freeing up space for leisure and relaxation. One effective technique is the Pomodoro method, where you work intensely for 25 minutes and then take a 5-minute break. This approach keeps your mind fresh and focused, preventing the burnout that comes with marathon work sessions. Eliminating distractions is also crucial. Whether putting your phone on silent or working in a quiet environment, minimizing interruptions helps you concentrate on the task at hand. It's about creating an environment where you can be your most efficient self, making the most of the time you have.

Activity: Build Your Dream Side Hustle

- Brainstorm: Grab a notebook or open a new document on your device. Think about your hobbies, skills, or interests. Do you love baking, art, or helping people? Write down three things you enjoy doing that could be turned into a side hustle.
- Create a Plan: Choose one of the ideas from your list. Now, write a simple plan for how you could turn this into a money-making opportunity. Consider who your customers would be, how you'd promote it (social media, word of mouth, etc.), and how much you'd charge.
- Promotion Design: a quick social media post for your side hustle! If you're an artist, showcase a drawing you've made. If you're interested in dog walking, use a fun photo of a dog. This step helps you think creatively about how to promote your new business.
- Presentation: Share your side hustle idea with a family member or friend. Get their feedback—would they hire you? Do they have ideas on how to improve your hustle? This step encourages you to think about your business from the customer's perspective.

As this Section wraps up, remember that balancing work and life is about making intentional choices. It's about creating a lifestyle that supports both your ambitions and personal well-being. By setting boundaries, managing your time wisely, and prioritizing your health, you set yourself up for professional and personal success. Finding this balance empowers you to pursue your goals with focus and energy, ready to tackle whatever comes next. As you master these skills, you're preparing yourself for a future that's not only productive but also fulfilling. Now, let's explore how you can use technology to enhance your financial journey.

Rafting down the Money River, we discover how to make money flow and grow, turning the current of our efforts into wealth.

SECTION 7: NAVIGATING PEER PRESSURE AND SOCIAL INFLUENCES

"Don't try so hard to fit in, and certainly don't try so hard to be different…just try hard to be you."

ZENDAYA

Picture this: your friends are all buzzing about the latest sneakers that just dropped. They're flashy and trendy, and everyone seems to have them. Suddenly, you feel that itch—the urge to buy them so you can fit in and not feel left out. This scenario is all too familiar, right? Peer pressure is a powerful force, especially when it comes to spending. Whether it's about snagging the hottest tech or keeping up with fashion, the influence of those around you can make it hard to stick to your financial goals. But don't worry—you're not alone in facing this challenge, and together, we'll explore how to navigate these tricky waters without sinking your budget.

~

SPENDING SMARTS: MAKING PURCHASES WITHOUT REGRET

It's all too easy to get caught up in the moment and make impulsive purchases you regret later. Try implementing a "24-hour rule" for non-essential buys to avoid this. The "24-hour rule" means giving yourself a whole day to think about whether you really need that item or if it's just a want. This pause can help you look at the purchase from all angles and decide if it's worth it. During this time, ask yourself, "Is this a need or a want?" Needs are essentials, things you can't do without, while wants are those nice-to-have items. This simple question can be a game-changer in keeping your spending in check and making sure your money goes to what truly matters.

Understanding the triggers behind impulsive buying can also help you make smarter choices. Marketing tactics are designed to make you spend. Ever notice those limited-time offers that seem too good to pass up? They create a sense of urgency, making you feel like you'll miss out if you don't act fast. Then there's the influence of peers. When friends rave about a product, it's hard not to feel the pull to buy it, too, and it is known as social proof, where we tend to do what others are doing to fit in. Being aware of these psychological triggers helps you recognize when you're being nudged toward an unnecessary purchase, giving you the power to resist.

To assess the true value of a purchase, consider its long-term utility. One method to try is the cost-per-use analysis. The cost-per-use analysis involves dividing the total cost of an item by the number of times you expect to use it. For example, if you're eyeing a $100 jacket and think you'll wear it 50 times, the cost-per-use is $2. Compare this with a $20 T-shirt you might only wear twice, which has a $10 cost-per-use. This perspective can shift your focus from the immediate appeal to the long-term value, helping you make more informed decisions about where to spend your money.

Setting personal spending limits is another strategy to keep your finances in check. Decide on a monthly discretionary spending cap—this is the amount you're comfortable spending on non-essentials. This boundary not only helps you control your spending but also encourages you to prioritize your purchases. If you've hit your limit for the month, it's a sign to pause and reconsider any further spending. These limits act like guardrails, keeping your budget on track while still allowing for some flexibility and fun.

Interactive Element: Reflection Exercise

Take a moment to think about your recent purchases. Were they needs or wants? Write them down, and for each item, consider its cost-per-use. Did it offer good value? Reflect on whether a "24-hour rule" might have changed your decision. This exercise will help you develop a habit of mindful spending and recognize patterns in your buying behavior.

With these tools and strategies, you're well-equipped to handle spending pressures wisely. It's all about understanding what drives your purchases and taking the time to evaluate their true value. By setting limits and considering long-term use, you can make confident decisions that align with your financial goals. Remember, spending smarts are not just about saving money—they're about making choices that reflect who you are and where you want to go.

∼

SOCIAL MEDIA AND MONEY: SEPARATING FACT FROM FICTION

It's easy to get swept away by the perfect lives seemingly everyone else is living when scrolling through social media. You know, the ones filled with endless travel, luxury items, and perfectly styled outfits. It's like a highlight reel of all the things we think we should have or be doing. But here's the thing: social media doesn't always show the whole picture. Influencers and celebrities often promote products through sponsored content, making it hard to distinguish between genuine endorsements and paid advertisements. This curated content can distort reality, leading us to believe these lifestyles are easily attainable, impacting how we perceive our own financial choices.

Learning how to evaluate online content critically is crucial in the information age. Start by researching influencer credentials. Are they experts in the field they're promoting, or are they just paid to say nice things? A quick search can reveal a lot about their background and legitimacy. Next, fact-check financial tips that seem too good to be true. Cross-reference advice with reputable sources or look for reviews from unbiased users. Remember, just because something is popular doesn't mean it's your best choice. By honing your critical thinking skills, you can sift through the noise and find the information that truly benefits your financial well-being.

Social media can also fuel the comparison culture, where we constantly measure ourselves against others. You might feel pressured to keep up with the latest trends or mimic the lifestyles of people you follow. The "keeping up with the Joneses" mindset can lead to unhealthy spending habits, as you might buy things not because you need them but because you feel like you should have them. It's easy to forget that what we see online is often a polished version of reality. People's lives are more complex than what they share on their feeds, and their financial situations are likely different from yours.

Instead of falling into the comparison trap, focus on following credible financial educators who offer real value. Many personal finance podcasts and YouTube channels are run by experts who provide practical advice on budgeting, saving, and investing. Some certified financial planners also share tips on social media, making financial literacy accessible and engaging. By tuning into these reliable sources, you can gain insights that help you make informed decisions about your money. It's about finding voices that guide you toward financial health rather than those that pressure you into spending more.

Interactive Element: Researching Influencers

Take a moment to pick a financial influencer or educator you follow online. Research their background and credentials, and look for reviews of their content. Write down three key points that you learn from this exercise. This will help you build a habit of critically evaluating the information you consume and ensure you're following trustworthy sources.

By understanding social media dynamics, you can navigate its influence with awareness and intention. It's about separating fact from fiction, recognizing the difference between curated content and reality, and focusing on what truly matters to you. As you become more mindful of the media you consume, you'll find it easier to resist the pressure to conform and make choices that align with your financial values and goals.

FOMO AND FINANCES: AVOIDING IMPULSE SPENDING

Ever find yourself scrolling through your feed, and suddenly you feel like you're missing out on the latest concert, the hottest sneaker release, or that epic trip your friends are planning? That uneasy feeling is called FOMO, or Fear of Missing Out, and it has a powerful pull on our wallets. It drives us to spend impulsively so that we can join in on the fun or keep up with what everyone else seems to be doing. This urge can disrupt our budgets and make it tough to stick to financial goals. FOMO can create a whirlwind of spending that leaves you wondering where your money went and why you bought things you didn't really need.

Start by practicing gratitude for what you already have to combat FOMO and its pesky influence. It's easy to forget the good things in our lives when we're constantly bombarded with images of what we don't have. Taking a moment each day to appreciate what's around you can shift your focus from what you're missing to what you're grateful for. This simple act can ground you, reducing the hold that FOMO has. Another strategy is to consider your long-term goals before making a purchase. Ask yourself if buying that trendy item will bring you closer to or further from what you truly want in the future. Sometimes, a little reflection is all it takes to make a decision that aligns with your bigger picture.

Reflecting on your personal values and priorities can be a game-changer in resisting FOMO-driven spending. Take a moment to think about what truly matters to you. Is it experiences over things? Saving for a big goal like college or travel? Align your spending with these values, and let them guide your financial decisions. Creating a personal mission statement for spending can be a helpful tool. This statement reminds you of your priorities, helping you stay on track when FOMO strikes. It might say something like, "I prioritize saving for experiences that enrich my life over purchasing material goods." This clarity can give you the strength to say 'no' to unnecessary spending and 'yes' to what truly matters.

Real-life success stories can be incredibly inspiring when it comes to overcoming FOMO. Take Tom, a teen who used to spend all his money on frequent outings and the latest gadgets just to fit in. He realized he wasn't moving closer to his dream of traveling the world. After reflecting on his values, he decided to save up for a study abroad program instead. By shifting his mindset, Tom managed to cut back on impulsive buys and focus on his travel goal. Each small sacrifice brought him closer to his dream, and he felt a sense of accomplishment that far outweighed the temporary high of buying new things. Stories like Tom's show that breaking free from FOMO and making mindful choices that lead to fulfilling outcomes are possible.

Reflection Section: Creating Your Personal Mission Statement

Grab a journal or open a notes app. Consider what truly matters to you and how you want your spending to reflect those values. Write down a personal mission statement about your financial priorities. Revisit this statement whenever you feel the tug of FOMO. This exercise helps clarify your goals and align you with what's most important to you.

FOMO doesn't have to control your finances. By understanding its impact, practicing gratitude, aligning spending with personal values, and drawing inspiration from others, you can make mindful choices that support your long-term goals. It's about finding balance and remembering that you don't have to follow every trend or attend every event to lead a fulfilling life.

~

SQUAD GOALS: ENCOURAGING HEALTHY FINANCIAL HABITS IN YOUR FRIEND GROUP

Imagine this: you and your friends are hanging out, and the topic of money comes up. It might feel a bit awkward at first, but discussing financial goals openly can be incredibly empowering. When friends talk openly about money, it helps everyone make better decisions. You can swap budgeting tips, share savings goals, and support each other in sticking to financial plans. For example, if you've found a great way to save on streaming services, why not share that hack with your crew? Likewise, hearing how a friend managed to save for a trip might inspire you to set a similar goal. These conversations can create a supportive environment where everyone feels comfortable discussing their financial wins and challenges without judgment.

When it comes to hanging out, you don't always have to break the bank to have a good time. Suggesting easy group activities on the wallet can be a fun way to bond while keeping spending in check. Instead of going out to eat at a pricey restaurant, why not host a potluck dinner? Each person can bring a dish, turning dinner into a diverse feast without anyone spending too much. Game nights are another great option. Dust off those board games or try out some new ones—it's a great way to laugh and enjoy each other's company without spending a dime. If you're feeling adventurous, organize a hike or a day at the beach. Nature offers some of the best free entertainment and a chance to create memories without a hefty price tag.

Group accountability can work wonders for staying committed to financial goals. Imagine setting up a savings challenge with your friends. Each of you could set a goal to save a certain amount by the end of the month. Whoever reaches their target gets to pick the next group activity. This keeps everyone motivated and adds a fun, competitive element to saving money. Another idea is to have budget-friendly challenges, like seeing who can find the best deals at a thrift shop or create the most stylish outfit for the least amount of money. These activities turn saving into a fun game, encouraging everyone to stick to their goals while having a blast together.

Sometimes, friends might suggest outings that are a bit too pricey. It's important to handle these situations tactfully. If a friend wants to go somewhere that's out of your budget, you can politely decline without feeling awkward. It's okay to say, "Hey, that sounds fun, but I'm trying to save money right now. How about we do something else?" By suggesting cost-effective alternatives, you show that you're still interested in spending time together, just in a different way. Maybe propose a picnic in the park or a movie night at home instead of an expensive dinner or concert. Your friends will appreciate your honesty and, more often than not, will be open to the idea.

Visual Element: Budget-Friendly Activity Ideas

Create a list of budget-friendly activities you can do with friends. Include options like potluck dinners, game nights, hiking trips, or thrift shop challenges. Keep this list handy for when you need inspiration, and share it with your friends to encourage more affordable hangouts.

Navigating financial peer pressure doesn't have to be daunting. By fostering open discussions about money, suggesting budget-friendly activities, and embracing group accountability, you can cultivate a friend group that supports each other's financial health. It's all about creating a community where everyone feels empowered to make smart financial decisions without feeling left out. Remember, true friendship is about enjoying each other's company, no matter how much or little you spend.

~

HANDLING MONEY DISCUSSIONS WITH FRIENDS: KEEPING IT COOL

When money topics come up, it can feel like walking a tightrope, trying not to ruffle any feathers or turn the vibe sour. Yet, diving into chats about cash with your crew can actually be super rewarding for everyone. The key is to approach these discussions with respect and understanding. Avoid comparisons or criticism, as these can lead to feelings of inadequacy or resentment. Instead, focus on listening and sharing experiences without judgment. Everyone's financial situation is different, and being sensitive to that can foster a supportive environment where you can all learn from each other.

Sometimes disagreements about money can arise, especially when friends have different spending habits or financial goals. It might be about how much to spend on a group outing or how to split costs fairly. Whatever the issue, addressing these disagreements with a mindset of compromise and understanding can go a long way. Start by acknowledging each other's perspectives and then work together to find a fair solution. Maybe it means setting a budget for activities or agreeing to take turns covering costs. Finding common ground helps maintain harmony in your friendships while respecting individual financial boundaries.

Setting clear boundaries around money is crucial, even among friends. It's important to be upfront about your budget constraints. If you're saving for something important, let your friends know. This transparency helps them understand your choices and prevents misunderstandings. You might say, "I'm trying to save up for a new phone, so I'm keeping a tight budget for now." By sharing your financial limits openly, you encourage your friends to do the same, promoting a culture where everyone feels comfortable discussing their financial realities without feeling pressured to overspend or fear being judged.

Think of financial education as a collective journey you can embark on together. Encourage your friends to join you in learning about money management. Consider signing up for financial workshops or online courses as a group. You can hold each other accountable and discuss what you've learned to reinforce the knowledge. Share resources and insights from your personal research, like a great book or podcast you found helpful. A shared learning experience not only strengthens your financial literacy but also deepens your bond as a group. It's about growing together and supporting each other in becoming financially savvy.

Money discussions with friends don't have to be awkward or uncomfortable. By approaching these conversations with respect, understanding, and a willingness to learn together, you can create an environment where everyone feels supported in their financial goals. It's all about lifting each other up and making sure nobody feels left behind. With open communication and shared growth, you and your friends can confidently and easily navigate the world of finances.

Quiz: Navigating Peer Pressure and Social Influences

1. What is the 24-hour rule for spending?
   a. Buying something immediately when you see it
   b. Waiting 24 hours before making a purchase to see if you really need it
   c. Asking your friends if they would buy it

2. What does "FOMO" stand for?
   a. Fear of Missing Opportunities
   b. Feeling Out of Money Options
   c. Fear of Missing Out
3. Which strategy can help you resist peer pressure to spend money?
   a. Only carrying cash so you can't overspend
   b. Ignoring your friends' opinions
   c. Reflecting on your personal financial goals before making decisions
4. What is "social proof" in the context of spending?
   a. When you spend money because your friends or influencers are doing it
   b. When you show your receipts to prove you made a good purchase
   c. When you buy something because it's on sale
5. How can you handle a situation when friends want to go somewhere expensive, but you're on a budget?
   a. Go anyway and worry about the cost later
   b. Politely suggest a more budget-friendly alternative
   c. Stop hanging out with those friends
6. What's the best way to evaluate if a purchase is a good idea?
   a. By considering its cost-per-use and long-term value
   b. By asking your friends if they have it
   c. By checking how popular the item is online

Answer Key

1. b) Waiting 24 hours before making a purchase to see if you really need it
2. c) Fear of Missing Out

3. c) Reflecting on your personal financial goals before making decisions
4. a) When you spend money because your friends or influencers are doing it
5. b) Politely suggest a more budget-friendly alternative
6. a) By considering its cost-per-use and long-term value

As this Section closes, remember that discussing money with friends is just one piece of the financial puzzle. Whether setting boundaries or learning together, these skills are building blocks for a financially independent future. Next, we'll explore how technology can boost financial success, offering tools and insights to enhance money management skills.

On the rocky terrain of Peer Pressure Peaks, we stay true to our financial path, avoiding distractions and staying focused on our goals.

SECTION 8: UTILIZING TECHNOLOGY FOR FINANCIAL SUCCESS

"The internet is becoming the town square for the global village of tomorrow."

BILL GATES

P icture this: you've just finished a long day at school and head home, excited to unwind. You plop down on your bed, phone in hand, and start scrolling through your favorite apps. Now, imagine if some of those apps could help you easily manage your money, turning your phone into a powerful financial ally. Welcome to the world where budgeting apps make financial management as simple as posting on social media. In this Section, we'll explore how technology can make budgeting not only easier but also something you'll actually enjoy.

Best Budgeting Apps for Teens: Managing Money on the Go

Let's kick things off by diving into some popular budgeting apps that are perfect for teens. First up is Mint, an app that's a favorite for its simplicity and effectiveness. Mint connects to your bank accounts, automatically tracking your expenses and categorizing them into neat little sections. It provides a clear snapshot of where your money is going, all in real time. Whether it's seeing how much you've spent on snacks this week or how close you are to saving for that new video game, Mint keeps you in the loop with minimal effort on your part. The app also lets you set budgets for different categories, sending you alerts when you're nearing your limit.

Next on the list is YNAB, which stands for You Need A Budget. This app takes a proactive approach to budgeting, encouraging you to plan for every dollar you earn. It's like having a personal financial coach in your pocket, guiding you to allocate funds for expenses, savings, and even a little fun. YNAB's philosophy is all about being intentional with your money and teaching you to prioritize your financial goals. It's a powerful tool for those ready to take a hands-on budgeting approach and learn valuable money skills along the way.

Then there's Goodbudget, which brings the classic envelope budgeting system to your phone. Imagine having digital envelopes for groceries, entertainment, and savings, each filled with a set amount of money. Once you've spent what's in an envelope, that's it—time to wait until the next refill. It's a straightforward way to ensure you don't over-spend, and seeing your "envelopes" empty is a great visual reminder to keep spending in check. Goodbudget is especially useful if you prefer a more tangible approach to managing your finances, even if it's digital.

You might wonder why you'd bother with an app when you could just jot things down in a notebook. Here's the deal: budgeting apps make tracking your spending and managing finances super convenient. They offer real-time updates, which means you can see exactly where your money is going as it happens. No more guessing or trying to remember where that $10 went. Plus, they provide visual representations of your financial data, like graphs and charts, making it easy to understand your spending habits at a glance. These features transform budgeting from a chore into a manageable, even enjoyable, part of your routine.

Choosing the right budgeting app depends on your personal preferences. Think about how much detail you want in your tracking. Do you prefer simple categories or want to dive deep into every dollar? Consider the app's compatibility with your devices. Some apps work better on specific operating systems or sync across multiple devices, which is handy if you use both a phone and a laptop. Take advantage of free trial periods or demo versions to test different apps. This way, you can find one that fits your style without committing right away. Remember, the best app is one that feels intuitive and meets your financial needs.

Experimenting with various apps is a great way to determine what aligns best with your financial goals. You might begin with Mint for an overview of your expenses, then shift to YNAB for more detailed planning. Or perhaps Goodbudget's envelope system feels just right. Each app offers a unique approach to budgeting, and trying them out can help you discover what feels like second nature. Consider it part of your financial journey—learning what tools work for you and how they can help you achieve your goals.

Interactive Element: Budgeting App Mini Challenge

Try out two different budgeting apps for a
  month each. Track your expenses and
  reflect on which app helps you manage your
  money most effectively. Consider aspects
  like ease of use, features, and how well it fits
  your lifestyle. Note down your experiences
  and which app you prefer, making it a fun
  challenge to boost your budgeting skills.
With these tools, managing your money
  becomes less daunting and more about
  making smart choices that lead you toward
  your financial goals.

～

FINANCIAL LITERACY ONLINE: LEARNING THROUGH DIGITAL RESOURCES

Imagine sitting in your room, laptop open, and having the world of financial knowledge at your fingertips. The internet is a treasure trove of resources that can help you navigate the complex world of money management. One of the standout platforms is Khan Academy, which offers free courses on financial literacy that are perfect for beginners. Whether you're curious about the basics of budgeting or want to understand credit, Khan Academy breaks down these topics into simple, digestible lessons. The platform's interactive exercises and video tutorials make learning engaging, allowing you to grasp financial concepts at your own pace.

For those who are ready to dive deeper, platforms like Coursera and Udemy offer in-depth finance courses taught by experts worldwide. These courses often come with certificates, which can be a nice addition to your resume. From understanding personal finance to exploring invest-ment strategies, these platforms cover a wide range of topics, making it easy to find a course that suits your interests and goals. The flexibility of online learning means you can fit these lessons around your schedule, whether it's a busy school day or a relaxed weekend. You get to choose when and how you learn, which makes education feel less like a chore and more like an adventure.

Another fantastic resource is Investopedia, a website that serves as a financial encyclopedia. If you ever come across a term or concept you don't understand, Investopedia is the place to go. It provides detailed explanations, examples, and quizzes to test your knowledge. This site is especially useful if you want to expand your vocabulary or explore more advanced financial topics. If you wish to know what "com-pound interest" means or how "diversification" works in investing, Investopedia has you covered. It's like having a financial dictionary right at your fingertips, ready to help you make sense of the financial world.

The advantages of online learning are immense, especially for financial literacy. The flexibility it offers is unmatched. You can learn at your own pace, pausing videos to take notes or rewatching sections that are tricky. This freedom allows you to absorb information in a way that suits your learning style, whether you're a visual learner or someone who prefers reading. Access to expert instructors is another bonus. Many of these courses are designed and taught by professionals with years of experience in the field. Their insights and tips can provide valuable guidance as you build your financial skills.

When diving into online resources, it's important to ensure the information you're receiving is accurate and reliable. Start by checking the credentials of authors or instructors. Look for qualifications or professional experience that lends credibility to their teachings. Reading reviews and testimonials from other learners can also give you an idea of the resource's quality. If many people found it helpful and informative, chances are you will, too. This step is crucial because not all information on the internet is trustworthy, and you want to make sure you're building your knowledge on a solid foundation.

Engaging with online financial communities can enhance your learning experience. Websites like Reddit have personal finance communities where you can ask questions, share experiences, and gain insights from others who are also learning about money management. These forums can be incredibly supportive, offering different perspectives and advice from people who have been in your shoes. Facebook groups dedicated to teen financial literacy are another great option. Joining these groups connects you with like-minded individuals who are eager to learn and grow together. It's a chance to build a network, gain motivation, and even make new friends who share your financial interests.

Resource List: Online Learning Platforms

- Khan Academy: Offers free financial literacy courses.
- Coursera and Udemy: Provides in-depth finance courses with certificates.

- Investopedia: A comprehensive site for financial terms and concepts.

These platforms are just the beginning. As you explore, you'll discover countless other resources to guide you on your financial learning journey.

≈

PROTECTING YOUR DATA: STAYING SAFE WHILE MANAGING MONEY

Managing money online is second nature in today's digital world, but lurking behind convenience is a risk that could catch you off guard if you're not careful. Imagine someone sneaking into your room and rifling through your personal stuff—pretty unsettling, right? That's essentially what happens when cybercriminals get hold of your personal information through identity theft or data breaches. When using financial apps or making transactions online, you're sharing sensitive data that needs protection, which is why safeguarding your personal information is so important. Losing control over your data can lead to unauthorized purchases or, worse, having your identity stolen, which can be a nightmare to resolve.

So, how do you keep your online financial activities secure? Start by creating strong, unique passwords for each of your accounts. Think of passwords as the keys to your digital house; you wouldn't use the same key for everything, would you? Use a mix of uppercase and lowercase letters, numbers, and symbols to make your passwords hard to crack. Also, consider using passphrases. These are longer, more complex passwords that are easier for you to remember but tough for others to guess. Enabling two-factor authentication is another smart move and means that even if someone has your password, they'd need a second form of verification, like a text message code, to access your account. It's an extra layer of security that can make all the difference.

Financial apps often come with built-in security features designed to protect your information. Look for apps that use encryption, which scrambles your data as it travels from your device to the app's servers. These make it difficult for hackers to intercept and read your information. Some apps also offer biometric login options, like fingerprint or facial recognition, which add an extra level of security. These features protect your data and make accessing your accounts more convenient for you. Knowing that advanced security measures shield your information can give you peace of mind as you manage your money online.

Awareness is your best defense against phishing scams and other fraudulent activities. Cybercriminals often use deceptive tactics to trick you into giving up your personal information. Be cautious with emails or messages that ask for your login details or payment information, especially if they seem urgent or too good to be true. These could be phishing attempts designed to steal your data. Always check the sender's email address and look for signs of impersonation. If something seems off, it probably is. Never click on suspicious links or download attachments from unknown sources. If you suspect fraudulent activity, immediately report it to the app's support team. They can investigate and take action to protect your account.

Staying safe online isn't just about relying on tech tools—it's about being proactive and vigilant. Regularly monitor your financial accounts for any unusual activity, and check your bank statements and transaction history to ensure every-thing looks correct. If you notice something unfamiliar, contact your bank or financial institution immediately. It's better to address potential issues early before they escalate. Keeping your software and apps updated is another crucial step. Updates often include security patches that protect against the latest threats, so make sure your devices are running the latest versions.

Visual Element: Online Security Checklist

- Create strong, unique passwords for each account.
- Enable two-factor authentication.
- Use apps with encryption and biometric login options.
- Regularly monitor financial accounts for suspicious activity.
- Be cautious with emails and links; report suspicious ones.

These steps might seem like extra effort, but keeping your financial life secure is worth it. You're already making smart choices by learning about money management, so adding these security habits can make your digital experience safer and more enjoyable.

~

SMART SHOPPING: USING APPS TO SAVE MONEY ON PURCHASES

Envision yourself wandering through your go-to store, fixated on snagging that dream handbag while still wanting to stash away some dough. That's where shopping apps come in handy, transforming your phone into a savvy shopping assistant. Apps like Honey, Rakuten, and Ibotta are game-changers for anyone looking to save money while shopping. Honey makes it a breeze by automatically applying the best coupon codes at checkout, ensuring you get the best deal without lifting a finger. Rakuten, previously known as Ebates, takes a different route, offering cashback on your purchases. You simply shop through their portal, and voilà, a percentage of your spending returns to your pocket. Then there's Ibotta, which gives you rebates on groceries and retail items. You can earn cash back on everyday purchases by snapping a picture of your receipt. Each of these apps is designed to ease the process of saving money, making your shopping experience smarter and more rewarding.

The allure of these apps lies in their ability to provide instant access to deals and discounts. You can uncover price reductions you might have missed otherwise at the tap of a screen. They even track price changes over time, helping you decide whether to buy now or hold off for a better deal. Imagine being able to shop confidently, knowing you're getting the best price possible. These apps do the heavy lifting, searching for discounts you might not even know exist. They help you keep more money in your wallet without sacrificing the things you love. It's like having a personal shopping assistant who's always on the hunt for the best bargains.

Maximizing savings with these tools involves a few strategic moves. Combining coupons with sale items can lead to double the discounts. Let's say you find a pair of jeans on sale, and Honey finds a coupon code for an additional 10% off. That's a win-win! Also, setting alerts for price drops on items you've been eyeing ensures you snag them at their lowest price. Apps like CamelCamelCamel can notify you when the price of a desired product on Amazon drops, allowing you to swoop in at the perfect time. These strategies take a little planning but can result in substantial savings over time, especially on big-ticket items.

However, one must tread carefully with the convenience of shopping apps, as the temptation to overspend is real. Online shopping makes it all too easy to add items to your cart without a second thought. To counter this, stick to a shopping list. It's your roadmap, keeping you focused on what you need rather than what catches your eye. This simple tool helps you avoid impulse buys that throw your budget off track. Setting a monthly spending limit within these apps also acts as a financial guardrail, preventing you from going overboard. It's about using these apps to your advantage while maintaining control over your spending habits.

Shopping apps can be a double-edged sword, offering convenience and savings but also the potential for overspending if not used wisely. It's all about balance, using technology to enhance your shopping experience without letting it lead you astray. Each time you refrain from an impulse buy or snag a great deal, you're honing your financial skills, turning shopping into a thoughtful, strategic activity. With the right approach, these apps can help you enjoy what you want while keeping your financial goals in sight.

～

TECH AND INVESTING: DIGITAL PLATFORMS FOR TEEN INVESTORS

Investing can seem like something only adults do—complicated, time-consuming, and a bit intimidating. But the truth is digital platforms have made investing accessible to everyone, including teens like you. Let's start with Robinhood, a platform that simplifies stock trading by eliminating commission fees. It's as easy as shopping online. You browse through stocks, pick what you like, and buy without extra costs. This app even allows you to buy fractional shares, meaning you don't need hundreds of dollars to start. Want to own a piece of a big company like Apple but only have a few bucks? No problem. Robinhood lets you invest with whatever amount you have, making it a perfect starting point for budding investors.

Then there's Acorns, which turns spare change into investments. Every time you make a purchase, Acorns rounds up the amount to the nearest dollar and invests the difference. It's like a digital piggy bank that grows with the market. You don't need to be a financial expert to use it, which makes it an inviting option for those new to investing. It's a set-it-and-forget-it kind of app that does the heavy lifting for you. Stash is another fantastic choice, offering beginner-friendly guidance and educational resources as you start your investing journey. Stash gives you the tools to learn about different investment options and helps you build a diversified portfolio. It's like having an investing coach right in your pocket, guiding you through the process.

Technology has truly transformed the investing landscape, breaking down barriers that once made investing seem exclusive. These platforms offer low-cost entry points, meaning you don't need a lot of money to start. They've democratized investing, providing everyone the opportunity to grow their wealth. Plus, they integrate educational resources, so you're not just investing blindly. Apps like Stash and Acorns offer insights into market trends and explain different investment strategies. This knowledge is power, helping you make informed decisions as you invest. With everything in one place—tracking, learning, and investing—

these platforms make the whole process streamlined and user-friendly.

When choosing an investment app, think about what you want to achieve. Are you interested in stocks or want to explore other options like ETFs or bonds? Consider the fees and commissions associated with trades, as these can eat into your profits if you're not careful. Some apps charge a monthly fee, while others might take a small percentage of each trade. It's worth comparing these costs to find the best fit. Also, look at the variety of investment options available. Some platforms offer a wider range than others, so if you want to diversify, make sure the app can support that. The right app should match your investment goals, providing the tools and resources you need to succeed.

Beyond just investing, these apps can become educational tools. Many offer virtual trading simulators where you can practice without risking real money, which is a great way to test strategies and gain confidence before diving in. You'll also find news feeds and analyst reports within the apps, which keep you updated on market trends and help you understand the factors influencing your investments. Engaging with these features encourages continuous learning, transforming you from a novice to a more seasoned investor over time. It's about building your knowledge and skills as you grow your portfolio.

As you explore the world of digital investing, remember that patience and learning go hand in hand. It's not about getting rich quickly—it's about making smart, informed decisions that build wealth over time. Investing is a journey, and these tools are here to guide you every step of the way. So, grab your phone, explore these platforms, and take that first step toward financial independence. Understanding how to make your money work for you is a skill that will serve you well throughout life. As this Section wraps up, remember that technology is your ally in financial success, making investing and managing money more accessible than ever. Transitioning to our next Section, we'll delve into the importance of crafting a future-ready financial plan, ensuring you're prepared for what comes next.

Quiz: Utilizing Technology for Financial Success

1. What does the app Mint help you do?
   a. Play music
   b. Track your expenses and set budgets
   c. Share photos with friends
2. Which budgeting app uses an envelope system to manage your spending?
   a. Mint
   b. YNAB
   c. Goodbudget
3. What is a key feature of the Acorns app?
   a. It plays games for you
   b. It rounds up your spare change and invests it
   c. It reminds you to pay bills
4. Why is it important to use two-factor authentication for financial apps?
   a. It makes logging in slower
   b. It provides an extra layer of security
   c. It lets you skip passwords
5. Which app allows you to invest in fractional shares of stocks?
   a. Robinhood
   b. Stash
   c. Both Robinhood and Stash

6. How can shopping apps like Honey help you save money?
   a. By finding and applying coupon codes automatically
   b. By limiting the number of items you can buy
   c. By hiding deals from you

7. What is the main benefit of using budgeting apps?
   a. They automatically earn you money
   b. They make it easy to track spending and stick to budgets
   c. They work like games for fun

Answer Key:

1. b) Track your expenses and set budgets
2. c) Goodbudget
3. b) It rounds up your spare change and invests it
4. b) It provides an extra layer of security
5. c) Both Robinhood and Stash
6. a) By finding and applying coupon codes automatically
7. b) They make it easy to track spending and stick to budgets

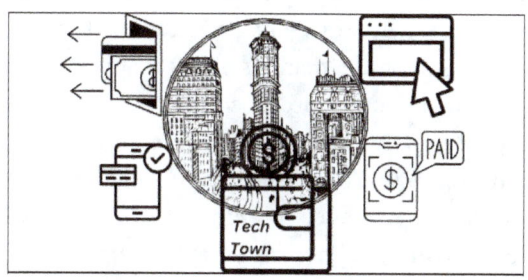

Reaching Tech Town, we arm ourselves with cutting-edge tools and apps, using technology to navigate our financial journey smarter and faster.

SECTION 9: CREATING A FUTURE-READY FINANCIAL PLAN

"You can't knock on opportunity's door and not be ready."

BRUNO MARS

When planning a road trip, you wouldn't just jump in the car and drive without a map or a plan, right? You'd consider where you're heading, the best routes to take, and perhaps even the stops you'll make along the way. Financial planning is a lot like that. It's about mapping out your life journey, ensuring you're prepared for the bumps and turns, and knowing exactly where you want to end up. So why not start planning now? You're setting yourself up for financial security and independence by thinking ahead. This isn't just for adults; starting early means you're giving yourself a head start, so when big life events roll around, you're ready to tackle them.

Let's say you dream of going to college, buying your first car, or even traveling the world someday. Each of these dreams has financial implications. How much will college cost, and what about saving for that car? Planning helps you see the bigger picture. It's about understanding what each life event might cost and preparing for them in advance. This foresight is crucial. It reduces stress and uncertainty because unexpected costs do not catch you off guard. Instead, you have a clear path and a plan to get you where you want to go. Think of it like having a financial GPS that guides you toward your goals, helping you avoid wrong turns.

A solid financial plan is like a toolbox that equips you with everything you need. It starts with budgeting for your daily needs and savings, which is your foundation, ensuring you're not just living paycheck to paycheck. Then, add in planning for taxes and insurance. While these might sound a bit daunting now, understanding them early on can save you from a lot of headaches later. Taxes affect what you actually take home from a job, and insurance protects you from life's unexpected events. When you include these elements in your financial plan, you're building a sturdy structure that can withstand the ups and downs of life.

Now, why is it so important to start planning early? It's all about creating habits, like brushing your teeth or exercising. Making financial planning a regular part of your routine sets you up for success. Regular financial reviews help you stay on track and adapt as your circumstances change. Maybe you start earning more, or your goals shift; flexibility ensures your plan always aligns with your current situation. Starting now also means you get to enjoy the benefits of planning sooner. You'll feel more in control and confident, knowing you're paving the way for a future that's bright and full of possibilities.

Interactive Element: Your Financial Roadmap

Take some time to create your own financial roadmap. Consider the significant life events you foresee, like college or buying a car. Write them down and estimate their costs. Then, map out the steps you'll need to take to achieve them, like starting a savings plan or researching scholarships. This exercise helps you visualize your financial journey and identify the milestones you'll need to hit along the way. It's a practical way to turn dreams into achievable goals.

∽

FINANCIAL GOAL SETTING: CREATING A ROADMAP FOR SUCCESS

Let's get real about goal setting. It's not just about saying you want to save up for something cool, like the latest tech or a dream vacation. It's about making those goals specific, measurable, and actionable. That's where the SMART goals framework comes in handy. Imagine setting a goal to save $300 by the end of the summer. That's Specific. You can track how much you save each week, making it Measurable. Consider if it's Achievable—are your earnings enough to hit that target? Next, think if it's Relevant—does it align with your interests or career goals, like buying a new laptop for school projects? Lastly, set a Time-bound deadline to keep you on track. This method transforms vague wishes into clear, actionable plans, making it easier to stay focused and motivated.

Think of financial milestones as stepping stones to your bigger dreams. Let's say you're saving for a new laptop. That's not just about the device itself but also about investing in your future, especially if you're into graphic design or coding. Each smaller goal you accomplish contributes to something greater. Maybe you start by saving money from a part-time job, then gradually increase your savings as you gain more confidence and resources. These milestones not only give you a sense of achievement but also provide momentum to tackle larger goals. They act as checkpoints, helping you assess your progress and adjust your strategy if needed. Celebrating these small victories keeps you motivated and on the path to your ultimate objectives.

Prioritizing your goals can be tricky but also exciting. With so many things competing for your attention, how do you decide what to focus on first? Start by laying out all your goals, both big and small, and create a timeline. Short-term goals, like saving for concert tickets, might take precedence because they're immediate, but don't lose sight of the medium and long-term goals like college tuition. Align these goals with different life stages. Are you planning to study abroad? Maybe that requires saving more aggressively now. Take into account your current income and find a balance. This timeline acts as a personal roadmap, helping you navigate through your financial landscape with clarity and purpose.

Flexibility is key when it comes to financial goals. Life is unpredictable, and sometimes priorities shift. You could land a better-paying job or discover a new passion that requires financial investment. Regularly reviewing and adjusting your goals ensures they remain in sync with your evolving circumstances. Don't be afraid to recalibrate based on changes in income, unexpected expenses, or new opportunities. This adaptability helps you stay on track and builds resilience, teaching you to manage your finances confidently. It's about being proactive, recognizing when adjustments are needed, and taking charge of your financial direction.

∾

PREPARING FOR BIG PURCHASES: SAVING FOR CARS, COLLEGE, AND MORE

Think about the excitement of buying your first car or heading off to college. These are big milestones, but they come with hefty price tags. Planning for these major expenses is crucial, and starting early can make a huge difference. When you plan ahead, you reduce the stress of large financial commitments. You're not just saving money; you're preparing for the total cost of ownership. A car, for example, isn't just about the sticker price. You need to think about insurance, maintenance, and gas. Knowing all the costs upfront helps you budget better, making the experience more manageable and enjoyable.

One effective way to save for these big purchases is to set up dedicated savings accounts to keep your money organized and your goals clear. You could have one account for a car and another for college expenses. Automated transfers from your main account make saving consistent and effortless. Setting aside a specific amount each month allows you to watch your savings grow without constantly thinking about it. This method is less stressful and ensures you're always moving closer to your goals. Over time, these small, regular contributions add up, bringing your dreams within reach.

Let's talk about opportunity cost. It's a fancy term, but it just means considering what you might have to give up by choosing one option over another. Say you're deciding between buying a new car or a used one. The new car is flashy, but the used one is cheaper, and the money you save could go toward college tuition. Every financial choice you make has a trade-off, which helps you make better decisions. It's about weighing the pros and cons and thinking long-term. Sometimes, the immediate thrill of a shiny new car isn't worth the financial strain it might cause in the future.

When it comes to big purchases, understanding financing options is key. Loans can be helpful, but they also come with interest rates and terms you must consider carefully. Comparing these rates can save you a lot of money in the long run. For example, student loans can be a good investment in your education, but it's essential to know the repayment terms before signing up. A low interest rate might seem appealing, but a shorter term could mean higher monthly payments. Balancing these factors helps you make informed choices that align with your financial goals.

～

LONG-TERM SAVINGS: UNDERSTANDING RETIREMENT AND BEYOND

Imagine thinking about retirement when you're still a teenager. It might seem far off, but starting to save for it early can make a huge difference. This is where the magic of compounding interest comes in. Picture your money growing over decades, like a snowball rolling down a hill, picking up more snow as it goes. Thanks to this compounding effect, the earlier you start saving, the more time your money has to grow. Even small contributions can become a significant nest egg if you give them enough time.

Employer-sponsored retirement plans, like a 401(k), are also a fantastic way to save. They often offer matching contributions, which are basically free money from your employer. Taking advantage of these plans as soon as possible is a smart move.

There are several options for retirement savings, each with its own perks. Traditional and Roth IRAs are popular choices. Traditional IRAs let you contribute pre-tax dollars, which can lower your taxable income now, but you'll pay taxes when you withdraw the money in retirement. Roth IRAs work the opposite way: you contribute after-tax dollars, but your withdrawals are tax-free. Deciding between them depends on your current tax situation and what you expect in the future. Many employers offer 401(k) plans, which allow you to save a significant amount each year, often with the benefit of employer matches. Understanding these options can help you choose the best path for your long-term savings.

Consistency is vital when it comes to building your retirement savings. Regular contributions, no matter how small, add up over time. Automating these contributions makes it easier to stick to your plan. Many banks and financial institutions offer services to automatically transfer money from your checking account to your retirement account. This way, you're saving without even thinking about it. This habit builds your savings and instills a sense of discipline and commitment to your financial future. It's like setting your finances on autopilot, ensuring you're always moving toward your goals.

Balancing your current expenses with the need to save for the future can be tricky. It's important to allocate some of your income to long-term savings while meeting your short-term needs, which might mean cutting back on some non-essential spending or finding ways to increase your income. For instance, you could aim to save at least 10-15% of your income for retirement, adjusting as necessary based on your personal situation. This balance ensures that while you're preparing for the future, you're also enjoying life now.

~

OVERCOMING FINANCIAL MISTAKES: LEARNING AND MOVING FORWARD

We all mess up with money sometimes. Maybe you splurged on something you didn't really need or forgot to save for something important. It happens to everyone. The key is not to beat yourself up but to learn from these hiccups. Over-spending is a big one. It's easy to get carried away, especially when something cool catches your eye. Then there's neglecting savings. You might think, "I'll start saving next month," but next month never comes. Scams are another trap; they can lure you in with promises that seem too good to be true. Recognizing these mistakes is the first step. It's like finding the crack in the foundation before it leads to bigger problems.

Once you spot a financial mistake, it's time to fix it. Let's say you've racked up some debt. Creating a debt repayment plan can help. Start by listing all your debts, then prioritize them —maybe focus on the one with the highest interest first. Paying off debt might mean making some sacrifices, like cutting back on extras, but debt-free relief is worth it. If an emergency wiped out your savings, focus on rebuilding. Set small, achievable goals, like saving $20 a week. It doesn't seem like much, but it adds up. Consistency is your friend here. Over time, you'll see your savings grow again.

Having a resilient mindset is crucial. Mistakes can feel huge, but they're just stepping stones. Reflecting on what went wrong helps ensure it doesn't happen again. Maybe you'll set stricter spending limits or research more before investing in something new. The goal is to learn and adapt. Stay positive and open to learning. Every financial setback is a chance to grow. Think of it like leveling up in a game—each mistake is an opportunity to gain new skills and strategies.

There are resources out there to help you on this journey of growth. Financial literacy workshops and online courses can provide valuable insights and skills. These resources offer a structured way to learn more about managing money. Sometimes, getting advice from a financial advisor can be helpful, too. They can offer personalized guidance based on your unique situation. Don't hesitate to reach out for help when you need it. There's no shame in asking for advice; it can make a difference in your financial confidence and competence.

～

TALKING MONEY WITH PARENTS: BUILDING A SUPPORTIVE RELATIONSHIP

Talking about money with your parents might initially feel awkward, but it can be super helpful. Think of it like having a team on your side. Your parents have been managing finances for years, so they've got a lot of experience and advice to share. By discussing your financial goals and challenges with them, you can gain insights that you might not have considered. Sharing how you're budgeting your allowance or saving up for something special can open up a conversation where you both learn from each other. These discussions can help you avoid potential pitfalls and make informed decisions. Your parents might even share their own budgeting and saving strategies, giving you a broader perspective on managing money effectively.

Starting a conversation about money doesn't have to be difficult. Timing is everything. Find a moment when everyone is relaxed, maybe after dinner or during a quiet weekend afternoon, which sets a more open and receptive tone. Use specific examples to illustrate your needs or goals. Instead of saying, "I need more money," try, "I'm saving for a laptop because it'll help me with school projects." This clarity helps your parents understand your perspective and makes the conversation more meaningful. Remember, it's okay to ask questions, too. If you're curious about how they managed their finances at your age or how they plan for big expenses, just ask. Their experiences can offer valuable lessons.

Parents play a huge role in financial education. They can guide you through the basics of money management and share their successes and mistakes. It's like having a personal financial coach. Learning from their experiences can build a strong foundation for your financial future. They might teach you about balancing a checkbook, understanding credit, or even the importance of a rainy-day fund. Their insights are invaluable, and they can help demystify complex financial concepts. Listening to their advice and applying it to your own life can prepare you for the financial responsibilities that lie ahead.

Working together with your parents on financial planning can also be beneficial. Consider collaborating on joint savings goals, like a family vacation or shared expenses. This teamwork approach fosters a sense of unity and shared purpose. It's an opportunity to see how financial planning works in real life and practice good habits. You'll learn to compromise, prioritize, and track savings progress as a team. Plus, achieving these goals together can be incredibly rewarding and strengthen your family bonds.

~

STAYING MOTIVATED: KEEPING YOUR FINANCIAL GOALS IN FOCUS

Staying motivated when working toward financial goals can feel like trying to keep a kite flying in a gentle breeze. Some days are easier than others, but maintaining your focus is key. One way to stay engaged is by visualizing the long-term benefits of reaching your goals. Imagine the freedom of not having to worry about money or the excitement of affording something you've always wanted. Keeping these end rewards in mind can act as a powerful motivator. It's also important to celebrate small milestones along the way. Every step forward, no matter how small, deserves recognition. The recognition can be as simple as treating yourself to your favorite snack or taking a moment to appreciate your progress. Celebrating these achievements makes the journey feel rewarding and gives you the boost you need to keep going.

Regular check-ins and reminders can help you stay on track. Set a monthly date to reflect on your achievements and challenges. This routine allows you to assess what's working and what might need tweaking. During these check-ins, review your goals and make note of any obstacles you've encountered. Were there unexpected expenses? Did you manage to save more than planned? Reflecting on these moments helps you adjust your plan and strategies. It's an opportunity to learn and grow, ensuring your goals align with your current situation. These regular reviews keep your vision clear, reminding you of why you started and where you want to go.

Setbacks are inevitable, but they don't have to derail your progress. When you encounter obstacles, approach them as learning opportunities. Maybe you overspent one month or didn't save as much as you'd hoped. Instead of feeling discouraged, use these experiences to adjust your approach. Did you underestimate your expenses? Could you find a more efficient way to save? Adapting your plan to fit new circumstances keeps you moving forward. It's about resilience and the ability to bounce back stronger. Remember, setbacks are temporary, and each is a chance to refine your strategy and continue your journey with newfound insight.

Hearing success stories from peers can be incredibly inspiring. Consider teens who have successfully saved for college or bought their first car. Their stories show that achieving financial goals with dedication and perseverance is possible. For example, a friend of mine worked part-time for several years, setting aside a portion of each paycheck. Eventually, she saved enough for a down payment on a car, which gave her a sense of freedom and independence. These real-life examples encourage you to push through challenges and remind you that your efforts will pay off. Remember these stories on days when motivation wanes, knowing that your hard work is paving the way to your own success.

~

CELEBRATING SUCCESS: RECOGNIZING AND REWARDING ACHIEVEMENTS

Imagine hitting that savings goal you've been working on for months or finally paying off a debt that's been looming over you. It's a big deal and something worth celebrating and recognizing your achievements, whether big or small, is vital to keeping your motivation alive. It's like giving yourself a pat on the back, acknowledging the hard work and dedication you've put in. These milestones are not just checkmarks on a list; they're proof of your ability to manage finances and stick to a plan. Celebrating these moments can boost your confidence, reinforcing the belief that you can handle whatever financial challenges come your way in the future.

But how do you celebrate without going overboard and undoing your progress? The key is to reward yourself responsibly. Set a small budget specifically for a treat or a personal reward. Maybe it's a nice meal, a new book, or even a special day trip. The idea is to enjoy the fruits of your labor without derailing your financial plans. By planning your rewards, you ensure they fit within your budget, allowing you to celebrate without stress. This approach gives you something to look forward to without guilt, making your financial journey enjoyable and sustainable.

Reflection plays a crucial role in understanding your financial progress. Take time to think about the journey you've been on, the lessons you've learned, and how you've grown. Journaling can be a great tool here. Write about your financial experiences, your successes, and even the challenges you've faced. This practice solidifies the lessons learned and provides a roadmap for future aspirations. It's a personal record of your growth, offering insights to guide your decisions moving forward. Understanding the process helps you appreciate how far you've come and prepares you for the next set of goals.

Once you've celebrated your success, it's time to set new goals and challenges. Financial growth doesn't stop at one achievement; it's an ongoing process. Look for new areas where you can improve or learn. Maybe it's exploring investment opportunities or understanding more about tax planning. Each new goal is a chance to expand your financial knowledge and skills. By continually challenging yourself, you maintain momentum and keep your financial journey dynamic and exciting. This forward-thinking mindset ensures you always move toward greater financial independence and security.

Activity: Create Your Own Financial Roadmap

In this activity, you'll design your personal financial roadmap to plan for your future financial goals. Think of this as your blueprint to success! Here's how to get started:

- Visualize Your Goals:
    - Grab a blank sheet of paper or use a digital app (like a notes or drawing app) and draw a long road across the page.
    - At the end of the road, list your "long-term goals," such as saving for college, buying a car, or traveling after graduation.
    - Along the road, list your "short-term goals" that will help you achieve your goals, such as saving $500 by the end of the year, starting a part-time job, or creating a monthly budget.
- Set Milestones:
    - Mark small milestones along the road that represent steps toward your bigger goals, such as

"open a savings account" or "cut down on non-essential spending."

- o Think about timelines: How long will each step take? Write estimated dates for each milestone.
- Add Fun Stops:
  - o Include fun "reward" stops along the way where you can celebrate small wins, like saving enough for a special item or reaching a specific savings goal.
- Share:
  - o Show your roadmap to a friend or family member, and explain your plan. Getting feedback or support can make the journey even smoother!

Quiz: Creating a Future-Ready Financial Plan

1. What is the first step in creating a financial plan?
   a. Buying something new
   b. Identifying your financial goals
   c. Spending all your money
2. What does SMART stand for when setting financial goals?
   a. Simple, Measured, Affordable, Realistic, Timely
   b. Specific, Measurable, Achievable, Relevant, Time-bound
   c. Short-term, Meaningful, Active, Realistic, Timely
3. Why is it important to start saving early for big purchases like college or a car?
   a. It reduces stress and helps you avoid last-minute scrambling
   b. Because everyone else is doing it
   c. So you can spend all the money right away
4. What is the opportunity cost in financial decision-making?

a. The amount of money you plan to save
b. The benefits you give up by choosing one option over another
c. A fee you pay for using your savings account

5. Why is it important to regularly review and adjust your financial goals?
   a. Because your goals will never change
   b. To make sure your goals align with any changes in your life or income
   c. To delete all your goals if they are too hard

6. What's a good way to stay motivated while working towards financial goals?
   a. By celebrating small wins and reflecting on your progress
   b. By ignoring your goals until the deadline
   c. By only setting unrealistic goals

Answer Key:

1. b) Identifying your financial goals
2. b) Specific, Measurable, Achievable, Relevant, Time-bound
3. a) It reduces stress and helps you avoid last-minute scrambling
4. b) The benefits you give up by choosing one option over another
5. b) To make sure your goals align with any changes in your life or income
6. a) By celebrating small wins and reflecting on your progress

As we wrap up this final Section, remember that financial success is not just about reaching a destination but also enjoying and learning from the ride. Each milestone is a building block in your financial foundation, setting the stage for even bigger achievements. With each success, you gain confidence and insight, preparing you for the next steps. Now, get ready to explore how to put these financial skills to work in real-world scenarios, bridging the gap between planning and practice.

Future Fortress

At the Future Fortress, we lay the final stone in our financial roadmap, preparing for a lifetime of stability and success.

CONCLUSION

"I'm not a businessman, I'm a business, man."

JAY-Z

Hey there, future financial whiz! We've journeyed through the ins and outs of money management, and I hope you're feeling a bit more equipped to tackle your financial future. We've covered everything from understanding the basics of budgeting to setting up your first investment account. By now, you should have a toolkit full of skills that can help you navigate the sometimes tricky world of finance.

Let's take a moment to recap some of the key insights we've explored together. You've learned how crucial it is to understand financial terms and concepts like budgeting, credit scores, and investing. These basics are your foundation. They help you make informed decisions and avoid common money pitfalls. We've talked about different income streams and how side hustles or part-time jobs can boost your earnings. We've also busted a few myths about money and highlighted the importance of setting SMART goals to keep your finances on track.

Financial literacy isn't just a fancy term. It's a life skill that empowers you to make choices that align with your dreams and values. It's about freedom—freedom to choose your path without being shackled by financial worry. This knowledge helps you build the life you envision, whether that's traveling the world, buying your first car, or simply feeling secure in your day-to-day life. Remember, being financially literate gives you the tools to shape your future.

Throughout this book, we've focused on practical skills you can use right away. Whether crafting your first budget, understanding how to use credit responsibly, or starting to save and invest for the future, these skills form the backbone of financial independence. Each Section has armed you with actionable steps and tips to apply what you've learned to real-life situations.

You've come a long way since page one, and that's worth celebrating! Every new term you understood, every budget you crafted, and every saving goal you hit marks your progress. It's important to acknowledge how far you've come. This journey isn't just about numbers; it's about growth, confidence, and the ability to gracefully handle life's financial ups and downs.

But remember, learning never stops. The financial world is always changing, and there's always something new to discover. Keep exploring, keep questioning, and keep pushing yourself to learn more. Whether diving deeper into investment strategies or learning about new digital tools, every bit of knowledge adds to your financial toolkit.

So, what's next? Take what you've learned here and put it into action. Maybe it's time to sit down and draft a financial plan or revisit your budgeting habits. Start small and gradually implement the strategies that resonate with you. Watch how these changes start to make a difference in your financial life.

Engage in conversations about money with your friends and family. Share what you've learned and invite them to join you on this financial journey. Talking about finances can sometimes feel awkward, but it's a great way to learn from each other and break down any taboos that might exist around money.

As you move forward, envision a future where you have the financial freedom to chase your dreams without hesitation. Whether starting a business, traveling the world, or simply living comfortably, your financial literacy will be your compass. You have the power to create a future that reflects your passions and aspirations.

Remember—you're not alone on this journey. I'm here cheering you on every step of the way. Financial independence is within your reach, and with the knowledge and skills you've gained, you can achieve it. Keep learning, keep growing, and most importantly, keep believing in yourself. You've got this!

UNLOCK THE POWER OF GENEROSITY

"True wealth is not in what we keep, but in what we give away."

UNKNOWN

Make a Difference with Your Review

Now that you've gained the tools to build confidence, strengthen your social skills, and start managing your finances like a pro, it's time to share what you've learned. Your journey doesn't stop here—it's just the beginning!

By leaving your honest opinion of *Smart Social and Money Skills for Teens*, you'll help guide other teens to the same support and encouragement you found, inspiring them to kickstart their own success.

Thank you for being part of this movement. When we share

our knowledge, we empower others to create a brighter future—and you're helping make that happen.

Thank you from the bottom of my heart!

Sydney Parker

ACKNOWLEDGMENTS

"The future belongs to those who believe in the beauty of their dreams."

SELENA GOMEZ

Thank you to my editor and illustrator, Chandni Ruparel.

I deeply appreciate your dedication and hard work in making this book the best it can be. The artwork featured in the book "Money Skills for Teens Made Easy" is her original creation. Any resemblance to other works, whether published or unpublished, is purely coincidental.

SOURCES

SOURCES FOR BOTH BOOKS IN THIS 2-FOR-1

The following sources have been referenced throughout both books in this 2-for-1. Each source supports content found across both works to provide comprehensive, reliable information for readers.

12 Best cash back apps for shopping, saving, and rewards. (n.d.). *Club Thrifty*. https://clubthrifty.com/best-cash-back-apps/

23 Best money apps for teens. (n.d.). *KidsMoney*. https://www.kidsmoney.org/teens/money-management/apps/

24 Ways teens can make money online. (n.d.). *GoHenry*. https://www.gohenry.com/us/blog/financial-education/24-ways-teens-can-make-money-online

5 Best freelance websites for beginners [in 2024]. (n.d.). *Austin Ulrich*. https://austinulrich.com/best-freelance-websites-for-beginners

5 Financial tips every young adult should know. (n.d.). *Petition Them*. https://www.petitionthem.com/5-financial-tips-every-young-adult-should-know/

5 Important credit card lessons for teens and young adults. (n.d.). *Sallie Mae*. https://www.salliemae.com/blog/credit-card-lessons-for-young-adults/

6 Real money lessons for teens every parent should teach. (n.d.). *EM People*. https://empeople.com/learn/empeople-insights/6-real-money-lessons-for-teens

7 Money myths to stop believing today. (n.d.). *Hudson Valley Credit Union*. https://www.hvcu.org/learning-center/7-money-myths-to-stop-believing-today/

8 Ways to help your teen build good credit now. (n.d.). *Experian*. https://www.experian.com/blogs/ask-experian/how-to-help-your-teen-build-credit/

American SPCC. (n.d.). *Encouraging positive online activities for kids.* https://americanspcc.org/encouraging-positive-online-activities-for-kids/

American University. (n.d.). *The importance of promoting digital citizenship for students.* https://soeonline.american.edu/blog/digital-citizenship-for-students/

SOURCES

Approve My Score. (n.d.). Understanding credit. *Approve My Score*. https://approvemyscore.com/blogs/b/understanding-credit

Banner Health. (n.d.). *8 ways to help your teen with social anxiety face the world.* https://www.bannerhealth.com/healthcareblog/advise-me/ways-to-help-your-teen-with-social-anxiety-face-the-world

Best savings accounts for teens (September 2024). (n.d.). *MarketWatch*. https://www.marketwatch.com/guides/savings/savings-account-for-teens/

Better Health Channel. (n.d.). *Teenagers and communication.* https://www.betterhealth.vic.gov.au/health/healthyliving/teenagers-and-communication

BrainyQuote. (n.d.). *Emma Stone quotes.* https://www.brainyquote.com/quotes/emma_stone_817700

BrainyQuote. (n.d.). *Emma Watson quotes.* https://www.brainyquote.com/quotes/emma_watson_615899

Budgeting tips for teens in 6 easy steps. (n.d.). *Better Money Habits*. https://bettermoneyhabits.bankofamerica.com/en/personal-banking/teaching-children-how-to-budget

Centervention. (n.d.). *Active listening exercises.* https://www.centervention.com/active-listening-exercises/

Child Mind Institute. (n.d.). *How to help your teen through a breakup.* https://childmind.org/article/how-to-help-your-teen-through-a-breakup/

Cole, J. (2014). *Love Yourz*. On *2014 Forest Hills Drive* [Album]. Roc Nation.

Coulbeck, P. (n.d.). Comparing Mint vs QuickBooks: Which accounting software is right? *The Free World Press*. http://marijuanaparty.fun/blogs/4785/16664/comparing-mint-vs-quick-books-which-accounting-software-is-righ

Cyberbullying.org. (n.d.). *Preventing cyberbullying: Top ten tips for teens.* https://cyberbullying.org/preventing-cyberbullying-top-ten-tips-for-teens

Designing a financial literacy program that works! (n.d.). *OBALearn*. https://www.obalearn.com/designing-financial-literacy-program-works/

ESC Region 13. (n.d.). *How to teach social skills through role-playing.* https://blog.esc13.net/how-to-teach-social-skills-through-role-playing/

Experian. (2020). *Why your credit score matters*. https://www.experian.com

Find financial literacy activities. (n.d.). *Consumer Financial Protection Bureau*. https://www.consumerfinance.gov/consumer-tools/educator-tools/youth-financial-education/teach/activities/

Finvision. (n.d.). Introducing emergency fund in 02 minutes. *Finvision*. http://www.finvision.in/introducing-emergency-fund-in-02-minutes/

Franklin, B. (1737). *Poor Richard's almanack*.

Gates, B. (1999). *Business @ the speed of thought: Succeeding in the digital economy*.

Goodreads. (n.d.). *Taylor Swift quotes.* https://www.goodreads.com/quotes/374278-just-be-yourself-there-is-no-one-better

Gomez, S. (2015). "The future belongs to those who believe in the beauty of their dreams." *Refinery29*. https://www.refinery29.com/en-us/selena-gomez-interview-dreams

Healthline. (n.d.). *8 breathing exercises for anxiety you can try right now.* https://www.healthline.com/health/breathing-exercises-for-anxiety

Healthline. (n.d.). *Positive self-talk: Benefits and techniques.* https://www.healthline.com/health/positive-self-talk

Helpful Professor. (2024). *38 examples of SMART goals for students.* https://helpfulprofessor.com/smart-goals-examples-for-students/

How are FICO scores calculated? (n.d.). *myFICO*. https://www.myfico.com/credit-education/whats-in-your-credit-score

How does compound interest work? Benefits of investing. (n.d.). *Halbert Hargrove*. https://www.halberthargrove.com/compound-interest-how-it-works-investing-early-benefits/

How does peer pressure influence your teen's purchasing. (n.d.). *Scripted*. https://www.scripted.com/writing-samples/how-does-peer-pressure-influence-your-teen-s-purchasing-choices

How FOMO impacts teenagers [2024 update]. (n.d.). *Axis.org*. https://axis.org/resource/a-parent-guide-to-teen-fomo/

How to deal with the peer pressure to spend more money. (n.d.). *Everfi*. https://everfi.com/blog/k-12/ideas-for-students-dealing-with-financial-peer-pressure/

How to give your teen constructive criticism. (n.d.). *Verywell Family*. https://www.verywellfamily.com/how-to-give-your-teen-criticicism-4086439

How to protect your data on money and budget apps. (n.d.). *Equifax*. https://www.equifax.com/personal/education/identity-theft/articles/-/learn/apps-cybersecurity-tips/

How to start a business as a teenager. (n.d.). *WikiHow*. https://www.wikihow.com/Start-a-Business-As-a-Teenager

Investing for teens: What they should know. (n.d.). *Investopedia*. https://www.investopedia.com/investing-for-teens-7111843

Jay-Z. (2005). *Diamonds from Sierra Leone* [Remix verse]. *Genius*. https://genius.com/Kanye-west-diamonds-from-sierra-leone-remix-lyrics

SOURCES

KidsHealth. (n.d.). *Rejection and how to handle it (for teens).* https://kidshealth.org/en/teens/rejection.html

Lady Wind Song. (n.d.). *The STAR method: A guide to mastering interview questions.* https://ladywindsong.com/5561-the-star-method-a-guide-to-mastering-interview-questions-51/

Lifehack. (n.d.). *15 highly successful people who failed before succeeding.* https://www.lifehack.org/articles/productivity/15-highly-successful-people-who-failed-their-way-success.html

Loveisrespect.org. (n.d.). *Self-esteem for teens: Why it matters, and how you can help.* https://www.loveisrespect.org/resources/self-esteem-teens-why-it-matters-how-you-can-help/

Mars, B. (2016). "You can't knock on opportunity's door and not be ready." *The Hollywood Reporter*. https://www.hollywoodreporter.com/news/bruno-mars-mans-world-interview-943495

Mayo Clinic. (n.d.). *Teens and social media use: What's the impact?* https://www.mayoclinic.org/healthy-lifestyle/tween-and-teen-health/in-depth/teens-and-social-media-use/art-20474437

Medical News Today. (n.d.). *18 mindfulness activities for teens and students.* https://www.medicalnewstoday.com/articles/mindfulness-activities-for-teens

Merriam-Webster. (n.d.). *Social anxiety.* https://www.merriam-webster.com/dictionary/social%20anxiety

Middle Earth. (2011, January 10). *How teens can be and pick a good friend.* https://middleearthnj.org/2011/01/10/how-teens-can-be-and-pick-a-good-friend/

Monash University. (2023, May 1). *Building a powerful self-identity: Why it matters for adolescents.* https://lens.monash.edu/@education/2023/05/01/1385697/building-a-powerful-self-identity-why-it-matters-for-adolescents

Moneywise America | Financial literacy for teens. (n.d.). *SchwabMoneywise*. https://www.schwabmoneywise.com/moneywise-america

Newport Academy. (n.d.). *Building resilience in children and teens.* https://www.newportacademy.com/resources/well-being/resilience-in-teens/

Office of Population Affairs. (n.d.). *Healthy relationships in adolescence.* https://opa.hhs.gov/adolescent-health/healthy-relationships-adolescence

OpenAI. (2024). *ChatGPT (GPT-4)* [Large language model]. Retrieved August 5, 2024, from OpenAI Platform.

Optima Living. (n.d.). Join the Optima Living annual food bank challenge: Building community through compassion. *Optima Living*. https://optimaliving.ca/blog/optima-food-bank-challenge

Parent and Teen. (n.d.). *Peer pressure: Strategies to help teens handle it effectively.* https://parentandteen.com/handle-peer-pressure/

Petition Them. (n.d.). *5 financial tips every young adult should know.* https://www.petitionthem.com/5-financial-tips-every-young-adult-should-know/

Pros and cons of using credit cards. (n.d.). *Credit Karma*. https://www.creditkarma.com/credit-cards/i/pros-cons-credit-cards

Raising Children Network. (n.d.). *Conflict management with pre-teens and teenagers.* Retrieved from https://raisingchildren.net.au/teens/communicating-relationships/communicating/conflict-management-with-teens

Raising Children Network. (n.d.). *Getting and giving sexual consent: Talking with teenagers.* Retrieved from https://raisingchildren.net.au/teens/communicating-relationships/tough-topics/getting-giving-sexual-consent-talking-with-teens

Rihanna. (2018, May). "I never thought I'd make this much money, so a number is not going to stop me from working." *Vogue*. https://www.vogue.com/article/rihanna-cover-may-2018

Self Financial. (n.d.). *Mark Cuban quotes: You don't need to raise money. You need to be smart and be focused.* https://www.self.inc/blog/mark-cuban-quotes

Setting a SMART savings goal. (n.d.). *FHI 360*. https://www.fhi360.org/wp-content/uploads/drupal/documents/cfpb_building_block_activities_setting-smart-savings-goal_guide.pdf

Smith, W. (2008). "It's not about how much you have; it's about how you manage what you have." *Forbes*.

Spark & Stitch Institute. (n.d.). *Teenage dating: Romance and the brain.* Retrieved from https://sparkandstitchinstitute.com/teenage-dating-romance-and-the-brain/

Start achieving your goals with SMART goals! (n.d.). *AirDoc Solutions*. https://airdocsolutions.com/sat/start-achieving-your-goals-with-smart-goals.html

T-Pain. (2019). "It's not about having a lot of money. It's knowing how to manage it." *Forbes*.

Teen guide: 5 steps to saving for something you really want. (n.d.). *Better Money Habits*. https://bettermoneyhabits.bankofamerica.com/en/saving-budgeting/saving-money-as-a-teenager

Teen Talk. (2012). *Role plays - Teen Talk.* Retrieved from https://teentalk.ca/wp-content/uploads/2014/05/Communication-Activity_TeenTalk-2012.pdf

Teens' guide to building a strong personal finance. (n.d.). *MoneyGeek*. https://www.moneygeek.com/financial-planning/personal-finance-for-teens/

SOURCES

The 50/30/20 rule for teens. (n.d.). *Banzai*. https://banzai.org/wellness/resources/fifty-thirty-twenty-coach

The 8 best budgeting & money apps for kids & teens. (n.d.). *GoHenry*. https://www.gohenry.com/uk/blog/financial-education/the-best-budgeting-apps-for-families

The Boston Banner. (2024). Strategies to help you save. *The Boston Banner*, 59(39), 10.

The impact of social media on teen spending habits. (n.d.). *Investors Cabin*. https://investorscabin.com/articles/the-impact-of-social-media-on-teen-spending-habits

Tilly's Life Center. (2022, October 25). *The mental health benefits of journaling for teens.* Retrieved from https://tillyslifecenter.org/2022/10/25/journaling-for-teens-mental-health-resources/

Top money apps for teens to start investing and budgeting. (n.d.). *Wall Street Zen*. https://www.wallstreetzen.com/blog/money-apps-for-teens/

Verywell Family. (n.d.). *How to give your teen constructive criticism.* Retrieved from https://www.verywellfamily.com/how-to-give-your-teen-criticicism-4086439

Verywell Mind. (n.d.). *10 signs of a toxic friend (and how to break up with them).* Retrieved from https://www.verywellmind.com/signs-of-a-toxic-friend-8430982

VirtualSpeech. (n.d.). *Examples of positive and negative body language.* Retrieved from https://virtualspeech.com/blog/examples-positive-and-negative-body-language

West, K. (n.d.). "Money doesn't grow on trees, but it can grow if you know how to invest it." *Goodreads*. https://www.goodreads.com/

What is compound interest? Explaining to kids and teens. (n.d.). *GoHenry*. https://www.gohenry.com/us/blog/financial-education/what-is-compound-interest-explaining-to-kids-and-teens

Wilde, O. (n.d.). *Be yourself; everyone else is already taken.* Widely attributed.

Zendaya. (n.d.). "Don't try so hard to fit in, and certainly don't try so hard to be different…just try hard to be you." *Inspiring Quotes*. https://www.inspiringquotes.us/quotes/jkIE_lgBDZIm7